GOOD HOUSEKEEPING
Needlecraft Is Fun

Book 1
Basic Sewing

written and illustrated by
Loraine Mirelle
B.Ed.

EBURY PRESS
LONDON

First published in 1975 by
Ebury Press
276 Vauxhall Bridge Road
London SW1V 1HF

ISBN 0 85223 054 0 (limp edition)
ISBN 0 85223 071 0 (cased edition)

Cover picture: Ginger Tilley

Printed Offset Litho and bound in Great Britain by
Cox & Wyman Ltd
London, Fakenham and Reading

Contents

Foreword

This is a book written especially for younger dressmakers, who expect instant fashion and do not want their clothes to last for ever and ever.

Nowadays anyone who sews her own clothes is forced to make a number of decisions which never troubled her mother nor her grandmother when they were learning to sew. The continual development of new textiles means that it is necessary to know the properties of the materials we choose, while the increasing use of modern sewing machines has made the choice between traditional and trade (or quick) methods another element in the generation gap.

The accent on technology has shown that if we are to make sensible choices it is very important to learn the new words needed before we can discuss our problems and learn from our decisions and experiences. One of the important contributions this book makes to our dressmaking is the emphasis it puts on language, both technical and aesthetic.

The text is full of commonsense, down to earth advice; if the economists' forecasts of world shortages come true and fabrics become scarcer and more expensive it will be increasingly important to plan our wardrobes most carefully and the collection of designs and techniques suggested in the 'Things to Do' sections will become a valuable guide to our choice of fashionable clothes within our budgets.

The information is broken up into useful chapters, each fully illustrated and planned for easy reference which should inspire the beginner with the confidence that leads to successful results and the discovery that needlecraft really can be fun.

MARGARET PERKINS
Senior Lecturer in Needlecrafts
Battersea College of Education

Introduction

This book is aimed primarily at the young beginner, although the not-so-young beginner may also find it useful. It is intended as a general guide to the processes of basic sewing and dressmaking, with the emphasis, wherever possible, on quick or quicker, methods rather than long laborious ones.

First, a word of warning. It is very tempting, when you long to start making your own clothes, to plunge straight in and take that first snip without really knowing what you are doing. But it is a great mistake to let your impatience get the better of you because early disasters can easily put you off sewing for life. Read Part One, 'Begin at the Beginning', first and it will tell you all you need to know about patterns, fabrics and equipment. That way your very first attempt will be a success. Part Two, 'Preparation Makes Perfect', tells you about fabric preparation, layout and cutting. Parts Three and Four show you how to assemble and fit the garment and Part Five deals with the later stages of neatening and finishing. The final part deals with those details which make all the difference to the finished article and shows you the right way to press the garment at each stage during its construction.

At the end of each main chapter there is a list of 'Golden Rules' to refresh your memory about the chief points in the preceding chapter. You will also find listed alphabetically some words and terms that may be unfamiliar and which are important to know. These are repeated, and defined, in the glossary at the end of the book (see note on page 242 explaining how to use the glossary).

Half the enjoyment of needlecraft lies in working out your own ideas on design and sewing techniques and, provided they work efficiently and the result looks good, there is no reason at all why you shouldn't experiment. The whole purpose of sewing and needlework is not just to copy and imitate the methods and ideas of others but to innovate and use your own imagination as much as possible.

LORAINE MIRELLE

KEY

SCISSORS SYMBOL ✂ This means cut, trim or snip fabric

CF Centre front to a garment

CB Centre back to a garment

FL Fitting line, or stitching line

WS Wrong side

RS Right side

cm Centimetre

m Metre

Begin at the Beginning

1. A Dress for All Seasons?

Providing clothes for your wardrobe takes money, skill, fashion flair and daring, in that order. Because money doesn't float from the skies and is often a problem when you are still at school or college, it is necessary to plan and budget. This means allowing certain amounts of money per week, month or year, for certain things.

Skill comes into the picture not only for making your own clothes, but also in knowing that some clothes are more functional for particular purposes than others, and that some clothes (co-ordinates especially) can lead a double life. Knowing your own self and how some clothes fit your personality and figure type best, is also partly a skill.

Fashion flair means knowing about colours, about patterns and about design and style.

Daring is needed to be able to wear fun clothes cleverly, lifting them from the merely gimmicky to high fashion, or to give your wardrobe a highly individual look.

Planning (fig 1)
At exactly the age (the early 'teens) when a girl wants to try out all the new fashions, she is often without a great deal of money. However, wonders can be achieved even with the smallest amount of pocket money.

The first thing to do is to make a list of all the clothes you've actually got in your wardrobe; include everything, starting with the main or large items first and ending with underwear and accessories (hats, bags, shoes, etc). Take a good look at the list when you've finished it and put a cross by any items which:

a you never wear, because you don't like them
b are so old even the moths aren't interested!

Look at the remaining items and list a few details about them at the side (colour, pattern, etc).

Figure 1   Figure 2

Now you can check if these items match up with or co-ordinate with anything else. If they do, you are probably a good wardrobe planner already – if they don't, you undoubtedly suffer from what is known as 'impulse buying' (buying on the spur of the moment). This is a trait you will have to curb a bit if you want a well-planned wardrobe within your budget.

Anyway, having checked this list, have a look at the items you have put a cross by. Could anything there be altered or adapted at all or is it all ready for the jumble sale or dustbin? (No sense cluttering up your wardrobe with stuff you don't want.)

When you have finished with list 1, start with list 2. This is the more interesting one. It consists of clothes you'd actually like (if you run out of paper it means you should start looking for a millionaire!). After writing it, check through and put a cross by items which are not absolutely essential at the moment.

Budgeting

Now have a look at the remaining items – how many are there? Are they major or minor items? Are they within your means in the near future or must you save for months?

List all the sources of income (pocket money, birthday money, etc) for about 3–6 months. The total will give you a long and a short range spending allowance. Divide this by 13 or 26 and this will give you an estimate of the weekly amount you can spend.

Figure 3

Figure 4

How much of this weekly allowance do you think you want (or need) to spend on clothes? Once you've decided on the amount, you have taken your first step to budgeting. Keeping within the limit is vital.

Work out the rough cost of each item of new clothing you need and whether you can reduce this by making it yourself. Remember that very gimmicky things should really be confined to the cheaper items as they date so quickly. You can budget in a number of ways:

a *The methodical but boring way*: For people who need to keep a strict routine. Put by the whole of your clothing allowance each week until you have enough money to buy the first item on your list. Repeat for item 2 and so on (fig 2).

b *The methodical but mediocre way*: For the whizz kid accountants with one-track minds. Allow so much each week of your clothing allowance for 5 or 6 items on the list (putting the money into separate jam jars, mattresses or wherever you hide it) and buy each item as you have enough money for it (fig 3).

c *The methodical but human way*: This suits most people and is the same as method **b** but allows an extra amount for impulse or gimmick buys. It also allows for the occasional lapse of spending every penny on a 'never-to-be-repeated' bargain (fig 4).

You know best how you work and whether you need the discipline of method **a** or the freedom of method **c**. Whichever way you

Figure 5   Figure 6

choose, try to keep to the list of items you actually need, as much as possible.

Skill

This is needed for making your own clothes, so saving yourself literally pounds and ensuring complete originality. A good basic pattern can be adapted in a number of ways to make a variety of clothes. Hunt around for fabric remnants and sale bargains both in the dressmaking and the furnishing fabric departments. (You can get some wonderful material in the latter and the extra width saves money.)

Adapt and alter clothes you already have so that they look completely different – go on, wield the scissors, be drastic. You've got nothing to lose and everything to gain. Turn a jacket into a sleeveless jerkin – a short skirt into a long one by adding multi-coloured frills – add trimmings – dye faded clothes in a sparkling new colour – add collars and cuffs to plain items – cut away armholes and necklines. As you see, the possibilities are endless.

FIGURE TYPES

Skill also means knowing your own figure and personality type when you are wardrobe planning. If you are *plump and short* (fig 5) you should avoid large patterns or patterns going around the body

Figure 7

Figure 8

(eg, horizontal stripes) and belts which cut your shape in two. Go for lengthways patterns (adding height), small all-over prints and the darker and more subtle shades of colour.

If you are *big-built* (fig 6) *and tall*, you can take larger patterns and more striking colours but try to keep the accents away from any large part of you, eg, if you have a big bottom, keep the bright colours and patterns above the belt and don't wear skirts too short (this makes you look even bigger round these parts). If you've a big bosom, wear plainer, darker and more subtle designs on your top half (and never wear lots of necklaces and pendants – these will make you look like a dowager duchess or an ageing barmaid!).

If you are *tall and slim* (fig 7) lucky you, almost anything goes. Layered looks are marvellous on you, as are trousers. Try to avoid the up-and-down beanstalk look by accentuating width, with belts, changes of colour from top to bottom, flares and so on. Any colours and patterns (to suit your own colouring, of course) and any fabrics such as chunky wools and tweeds, look great.

If you are *slim and tiny* (fig 8) you have as much of a problem as your short plump sisters, because big patterns swamp you and too bright or garish colours could make you look more like a butterfly than a 'bird'. Scale down patterns and styles to suit your size. Tiny patterns – clear, medium-toned colours, non-fussy styles, co-ordinates look good on you in toning colours and give you the definition you need to be noticed in a crowd.

PERSONALITY TYPES

As well as figure types, there are *personality* types to take into consideration. Are you a tomboy leading a very active life, happiest in jeans or trousers, or are you the ultra-feminine type who enjoys nothing better than swanning around in long and floaty clothes? Or are you a mixture of both of these, and it very much depends on your mood, how you dress?

This is where knowing something about the *function* of clothes is important. It is nice to have enough clothes in your wardrobe to suit whatever mood you are in but it is better to have the right clothes for the purposes you are going to need them for. Apart from school uniforms (which at least save your best clothes from getting worn out) you'll probably need some clothes to suit an active life. This means trousers, trouser suits (or matching tops) and co-ordinated clothes, eg, a skirt, trousers and jacket in same fabric and colour with toning sweaters and shirts or contrasting blouses. It is also advisable to have at least one dress or long skirt and top (they need not be frilly) for parties and special occasions just to remind the boys that you are a girl.

If you're a shy, retiring violet, then your clothes are probably simple and unostentatious: but you could liven things up a bit with (and get a lot of wear from) more interesting garments. An embroidered caftan or a peasant-look skirt and blouse are great for those special evenings with friends, without looking too dressed up (fig 9).

Figure 9

If you are a romantic kind of girl then you have probably got a lot of dresses already but you can't wear long floating skirts while riding a bike (too dangerous), cleaning the boyfriend's car (too mucky), or going for a job interview (might give the wrong impression). So a pair of jeans for the first two activities and a shorter length suit or dress (or trouser suit) for the second, will be needed.

If your parents buy most of your clothes and refuse to spend money on fashion gimmicks, use pocket money on fabric remnants and make your own fun clothes.

Fashion flair
This means knowing about colour, pattern, style and design, and using all the bits of information in a clever and effective way. Try to look at as many fashion magazines and 'glossies' as you can. If you can't afford to buy them, get your teacher at school to order them or club together with some friends and share them.

Look at the fashions, don't just sit there and yearn over beautiful but madly expensive clothes. Find out how you can imitate or adapt a look to suit yourself. That model who looks so good – is it the outfit, the accessories or the colours she is wearing which make it so? Collect fashion pictures and photographs and stick them in your own personal scrap book for future reference when you are deciding what to wear or make.

Colour
Colour is one of the most important parts of our lives and without it, it would be a very dull world indeed. Psychologists tell us that colour impresses our senses so much that it can affect us physically and mentally. The colour spectrum (which is really only the amount of light reflection or absorption of things), ranges from the warm colours, red, orange, brown and black (which absorb a great deal of heat) through the medium ones, yellow and purple, to the cooler ones, blue, green and white. We all know that on a hot day someone wearing a black or bright red dress will look hotter than she perhaps actually is (it makes us feel hot too) but someone in blue, green or white will look cool even if she doesn't feel it (fig 10). Actually white reflects back all the heat and light so therefore really *is* cooler. Conversely, in winter, wearing warm colours gives an artificial impression of warmth, and wearing a cool colour such as blue will probably just draw attention to a blue nose!

Subtle, muddy colours (like those used by Biba and Mary Quant) can look sophisticated and interesting, giving the wearer a look of expensive mystery, but they don't suit everyone – so be careful!

Figure 10

Colours for clothes should be chosen with a basic wardrobe and your own colouring in mind. If you choose a basic colour (or shades and tones of it) for the major items in your wardrobe, you will give a double life to your clothes because the permutations (mixing and matching) are then trebled. Extra colour can be added or introduced by the use of cheaper items, scarves, T-shirts, etc.

Your own colouring (skin, eyes, hair) should also be taken into account (fig 11). If you have *red hair* for instance, stay clear of reds, oranges and pinks, unless the shade exactly matches or tones with your hair. (Clever you – if you can do it!) Instead, go for the neutrals and natural colours – greys, browns, creamy colours, camel and so on; or for a contrast, yellows, blues and greens. Black and white can look really stunning on redheads too.

If you have *brown or black hair* then you should be able to wear most colours (fig 12). Take into account your skin colour of course. Brighter colours make a good contrast with your hair.

If you are *blonde, fair or mousey* blues, greens, browns and all pastel shades look right on you (fig 13). Yellow and orange can make blonde hair look brassy, so be wary. Red too, can make you look hard, so choose softer shades of red, eg, strawberry, if you like to wear it. Mousey hair can be livened up with rich jewel colours; purple, emerald, amethyst, ruby red, topaz yellow, turquoise, etc.

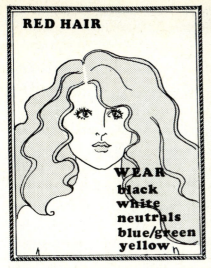

Figure 11

Figure 12

Skin colour can be temporarily changed by the skilful use of make-up so if you have a hankering for a colour you cannot normally wear, try altering your make-up colouring (if you wear it) as it can make quite a difference.

Pale skins look best with medium-toned colours. If you want to look really interesting at a party, pale skin can look marvellous

Figure 13

contrasted against a soft black fabric, such as black velvet – but do try to add a bit of colour and shine to lips and eyes, otherwise you could end up looking like a refugee from a horror movie!

Sallow skins – yellowish brown. These skins can be made to look slightly warmer, by wearing a touch of blusher or colour on the cheeks. To avoid looking jaundiced, never wear colours which emphasize the yellow, eg, acid green, yellow, etc. Keep to clear warm colours and mixtures.

Dark skins: Lucky you, as you can wear almost any colour; black too, can look really sophisticated against a dark skin. For impact though, try bright blues, pinks or yellows, and brilliant multi-coloured prints for evening wear to make you look exotic.

It would be a good thing if we could all get away from this dreadful habit of reverting to dark colours as soon as the winter arrives. All summer we sparkle in bird-of-paradise colours, then as soon as the nights get longer out come the sombre clothes. One could understand this years ago when winter clothes weren't washable, so had to be dark to avoid showing the dirt, but now with all the marvellous wash-and-wear fabrics around, why do we need to carry on this worn-out tradition?

Join the campaign against a grey world, spread a little colour about. It doesn't need to be overdone. Rich autumn colours for instance (the kind you find in leaves which have fallen from the trees) look lovely made up in wools and tweeds. Golden yellows and dusky pinks are practical for winter made in washable corduroys. Be adventurous with colour, make it a bright and beautiful world!

PATTERN

As we said before, pattern can make a difference to your shape. The general rule is: large patterns for large people (except the very plump), small patterns for small people, widthways patterns (horizontal stripes etc) for the skinnies and lengthways patterns (vertical stripes etc) for the fatties.

As well as choosing a pattern for your figure type, choose a pattern to emphasize the style (fig 14). For example, a smart, efficient style of dress looks good made up in a neat geometric print or crisp stripes; a romantic, floating dress looks nice made in an Art Nouveau type print (stylized flowers); peasant blouses or skirts look right made up in patchwork, gingham checks or small prints (choose different prints if you like, but co-ordinate the colours).

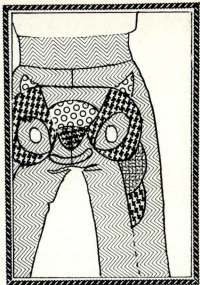

Figure 14   Figure 15

Patterns add interest. Try a patterned collar or belt on a plain dress, patterned turn-ups to trousers, pattern patches in special places such as knees, elbows or bottom for fun (fig 15). This brings us to the last essential in wardrobe planning.

Cutting a dash
You may look well dressed and neat, your clothes may fit their function, but without a dash of daring the total effect could be mediocre to the point of being boring. Wardrobe planning is a serious business only so far as the basic items and budgeting are concerned. As for the rest, it should be fun. So be brave. When you are young you can get away with more gimmicks and startling fashion than at any other time of your life. If you want to add strips of fur or feathers to the hems of tweed trousers and a couple of metres of the same slung around your neck (fig 16), go ahead. Anything goes if it works (that is, if the effect is good) and if you've the courage to wear it. The bizarre can be beautiful!

Ready to go
Once you've embarked on your plan for being the best dressed girl in your circle, you will probably realize that the easiest way of doing this on a limited income is to make your own clothes. The

Figure 16

following chapters are introduced to give you a working knowledge of patterns and fabrics. Unless you really understand these basic facts you may well never become a successful dressmaker. Trying to make clothes without mastering these simple elements would be like trying to build a house knowing nothing about bricks and mortar.

Words and terms used in this chapter
(see Glossary, page 242, for meanings)

accents	co-ordinates	mediocre
all-over pattern	discriminating	permutations
Art Nouveau	efficient	sombre
bizarre	estimate	sophisticated
budget	exotic	stylized
colour contrasts	function(al)	subtle
colour shades	gimmick(y)	trait
colour tones	garish	unostentatious
conversely	jaundiced	

Things to do
1 Design a new winter or summer wardrobe for yourself, listing items, fabric choice, colour, pattern, etc.
2 Choose a friend in your class and list a wardrobe of clothes to suit

her, giving reasons. (Compare notes afterwards – you may be surprised at the results!)

3 Bring all your old, unwanted (but clean) clothes into school and do a swop session or hold a sale (get permission first). Proceeds could go to charity or the school funds.

4 Collect together scraps of fabric in toning or contrasting colours and patterns and mount these in a scrap book. Note which colours go best together.

◎　◎　◎

2. All About Patterns

Before you make any garment you will have to choose a pattern to make it from (unless you make your own, in which case you will be advanced enough to skip this chapter). This entails knowing a little about pattern sizing and figure types. The reason for this is that it isn't always enough to go into a shop and buy a pattern by size alone, although many people do just this. It *may* not fit you and might need drastic alteration before it does. The following information should assist you in choosing the right pattern for your size and figure type.

Pattern size (fig 17)

This is really the sizing based on *widthways* measurements. A size 12 pattern, for example, would mean that it is meant to fit an 86 cm (34 in) bust and 91 cm (36 in) hips. When you buy a pattern by size you should first take your own measurements (see page 23) then buy the nearest pattern size to your bust measurements (for a dress, coat or jacket) and the nearest pattern size to your waist measurement (for a skirt or trousers).

If your hip measurement is more than 5 cm different from the correct pattern size waist measurement (trousers, skirts, etc) then buy by hip measurement and adjust accordingly.

If you measure an in-between size, choose the next size up or down depending on whether you like a tight or a loose fit; actually you can always slightly alter the pattern to accommodate this. Some patterns give such a lot of room for movement that you may even find by experience that you need a smaller size in certain brands!

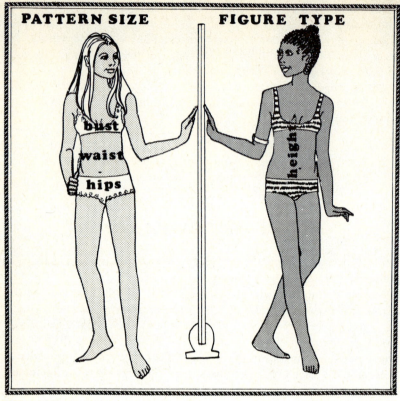

Figure 17

However, most good patterns should be cut to fit the size they say, plus a few cm extra for ease of movement. Commercial patterns vary from children's sizes to the largest ladies' sizes, with many pattern manufacturers making half sizes. This brings us on to the next point, figure types.

Figure types (fig 17)
When you have found out your basic measurements, you will probably see that some patterns give the back bodice length, skirt length and so on. If this seems confusing just take your own measurements and compare them with those of the pattern. Some pattern manufacturers make as many as seven different figure types ranging from 'chubby teenagers' to 'junior misses', etc.

Figure types are really based on *lengthways* measurements: the back waist length and the height of the individual. Short-waisted people may well find that the pattern size they want is a 'half size' or a 'junior petite'. Long-waisted people who are fairly tall may find they need 'women's' or 'misses' sizing. Children should never have scaled-down adult patterns, but patterns designed especially for children, which will cater for their various podges and general shapelessness.

Taking measurements (fig 18)
Before you buy another pattern, take your body measurements and keep a record of them on a card which you can keep in a safe place. The measurements you may find useful to take are as follows:

1 *Bust*: Measure over fullest part without pulling tape measure too tightly (not shown on chart below).

2 *Waist*: Around natural waistline, again not too tightly.

Figure 18

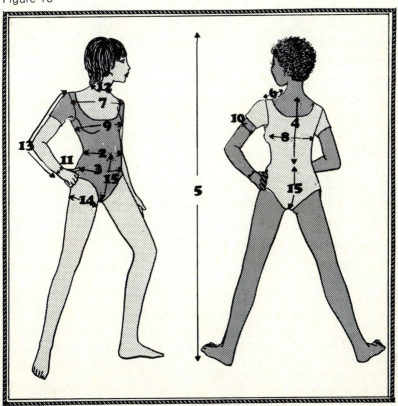

3 *Hips*: About 18–20 cm down from waist or over widest part of bottom (whichever is the larger).

4 *Back waist length*: Measure from nape of neck (the bone that juts out at the base of the neck) to middle part of natural waistline.

5 *Height*: Without shoes; measure from heels to top of head.

These are all the measurements you will need to know to buy a pattern. However, the following measurements are also useful for checking against the measurements of the actual paper pattern, after you have bought the nearest size to your own.

6 *Shoulder length*: From base of neck to shoulder point as far as where the armholes usually come.

7 *Shoulder width*: From shoulder across to shoulder at the widest part.

8 *Back measurement*: Measure across from underarm seam to underarm seam at shoulder-blade level.

9 *Front measurement*: Measure across bust from underarm seam to underarm seam.

Note: These last two measurements added together should be the same as the bust measurement. If the front measurement is more than 5 cm greater than the back measurement it means you have a full bust and should alter the pattern pieces to allow for this (see pages 27, 29, 30).

10 *Upperarm*: Measure around the fullest part.

11 *Wrist*: Measure around wrist bone but not too tight.

12 *Neck*: This is an important measurement for fitting collars etc.

13 *Length of sleeve*: Measure from top of shoulder to wrist, bending arm slightly and taking tape measure over the bend.

14 *Thigh measurement*: Essential for making trousers; measure the top of the thigh at the thickest part.

15 *Crotch measurement*: Pin end of tape measure to underneath seam join of a pair of trousers that fit well, and sit down. Get a friend to tell you the size marked off at the centre back waistline. Do the same with the front crotch measurement.

Any other measurements are up to you: you may decide to have a competition measuring ear size, but as woolly ear muffs are not often made to fit, it could be a waste of time!

◎ PATTERN ALTERATIONS ◎

If you have chosen a pattern as near to your own measurements and figure type as possible there shouldn't be a great deal of alteration to do. However, the best thing to do even before laying the material out, is to check that your own measurements (those listed) coincide with those on the pattern (allow a few cm for ease). If they do then you can carry on laying out the pattern on the fabric. If they don't, then alter the pattern to fit. A pattern can be adjusted anything up to 5 cm in size but if the alteration needs to be more than this, then it is better to buy the next size up or down and adjust this instead.

Lengthening or shortening
Some commercial patterns give marks where the adjustments can be made; if not, follow these instructions:

Bodice (of dress, blouse or jacket)
Mark centre of bodice between underarm and waist. Draw a line across pattern at right angles to straight grain (see chapter 5) at this level.

To lengthen, cut through this line. Place piece of tissue or paper under cut. Pull two pieces of pattern evenly until they are the desired amount apart, to give the extra length. 'Sellotape' pieces down to spare paper. Trim away excess spare paper at back. This will give new pattern length (fig 19a).

To shorten, fold paper pattern along the line. Crease into an even pleat so pattern is shortened by the desired amount. Pin in place or stick down (fig 19b).

Skirt
Mark off a point about a third of the way between hip level and hem. Draw a line at this mark at right angles to the straight grain across pattern piece.

To lengthen, cut through line and repeat instructions as for lengthening bodice (fig 20a).

To shorten, fold at this line and repeat instructions as for shortening bodice (fig 20b).

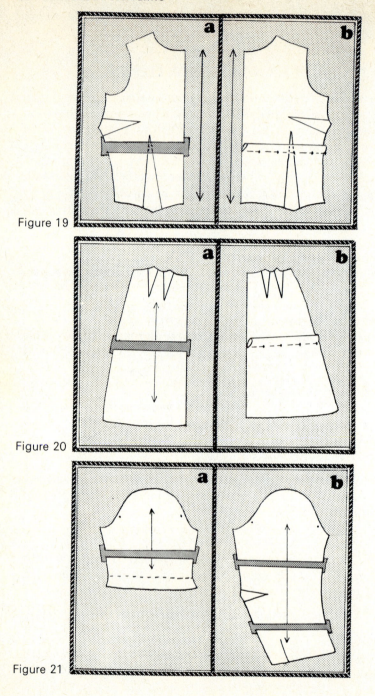

Figure 19

Figure 20

Figure 21

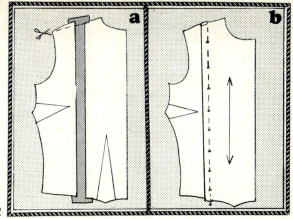

Figure 22

Sleeves

Mark off a point just above or below elbow dart (which comes exactly below point of elbow) and draw a line across at right angles to straight grain. If there is no elbow dart, choose a point midway between top of sleeve and elbow (short sleeves) and shorten or lengthen by required amount at this point (fig 21a). If it is a long sleeve it may need to be altered below the elbow as well as above it (fig 21b). If you are making two alterations to a sleeve remember that each will only be *half* the total amount of alteration required.

Widening or narrowing patterns

Sometimes it is necessary to adjust the width of the pattern. The following instructions tell you how to do this.

Bodices

Find point which is between edge of shoulder and neckline; mark it. Draw line parallel to straight grain (lengthways) down to waist level and adjust on this line by adding paper or folding a crease as for lengthening a bodice (figs 22a and b). Only half or quarter width of total adjustment need be made. (See * page 29.)

Skirts

Find point which is halfway between side seam and centre front (or back if this is the case) and mark it. Draw a line parallel from this point to straight grain down to hem level. Adjust width at this line, making only half or quarter width of finished adjustment (see * page 29) (figs 23a and b).

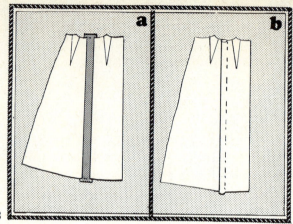

Figure 23

Sleeves

Draw a line parallel to straight grain from centre of sleeve head to hem of sleeve. Adjust this line (fig 24).

After you have made any adjustments, you may notice that the fitting lines no longer follow smoothly, in which case you will need to draw in new ones. Try to keep any curves as smooth as possible and draw any straight lines with a ruler (fig 25).

Figure 24

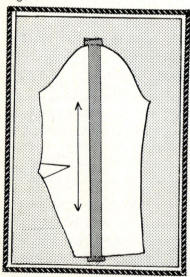

Figure 25

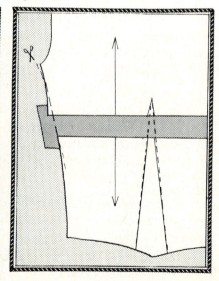

* Don't forget too, that if you make any *widthways* adjustments that you will have to take into account how many times the pattern piece is to be cut to make up the garment, and how many other pieces make up the width. This will make a difference to the amount you must take in or let out on each piece. For instance, if you wish to enlarge a bodice by an overall 6 cm, and the bodice has a pattern piece for half the front (to be placed to a fold) and for half the back (to be cut twice) then each piece should only be enlarged by 1·5 cm, because you will in fact be making *four* alterations and 4 × 1·5 cm = 6 cm: Or supposing you merely want to alter the back bodice by 3 cm, then cut the front pattern as normal, but alter the back pattern piece by 1·5 cm (2 × 1·5 cm = 3 cm).

Stop and think before you make any alterations and if necessary jot it down on a piece of paper. Small sketches of the pattern pieces with the adjustments written on them also help.

Other pattern alterations
Waist measurements
If you want to increase or decrease the waist measurement without altering the rest of the garment, do as follows:
1 Decide how much is to be altered and check how many pattern pieces you have which have a waistline and whether these pieces are to be cut double or not.
2 If you have two pattern pieces for the bodice, which have to be cut double, then the waist alteration amount should be divided by four. This will give the exact amount to adjust on each part of the seam, eg, to enlarge a waist by 2 cm alter side seam of each pattern piece by 0·5 cm (4 × 0·5 cm = 2 cm).
3 Add or subtract this amount to each side of pattern at waistline, following down a nice smooth curve to hipline for a skirt, or a fairly straight line for bodice (for increasing, see fig 26a). For very large alterations you may have to adjust waist darts also. Alter amounts accordingly, eg, to decrease skirt waistline by 5 cm which has two seams and six darts, remove 0·5 cm from each side seam (on all pattern pieces, making 2 cm) and approximately 0·5 cm from each dart, making 3 cm (5 cm in all). It sounds complicated but when you actually work it out it is fairly simple (fig 26b).

Shoulder length
If you have wide or narrow shoulders then the chances are that you will have to alter the shoulder seam measurement (wrinkles forming across the neck give an indication). If you do need to

change it then don't forget you may have to alter the sleeve head too, to make up for it. If you make the shoulder length shorter, then the sleeve head may have to be enlarged slightly. If you make it longer, the sleeve head may have to be made slightly smaller.

Adjusting for narrow shoulders (shortening)

1 Measure off shoulder length on bodice front pattern from neck edge to shoulder point, the length you require (if this is more than 2 cm larger or smaller you may need a different size pattern or figure type).
2 Mark new fitting line from this point in a gentle curve around to same underarm level as on original pattern. Repeat with back bodice (fig 27a).
3 Cut pattern, *not on this line* but *parallel to this line* the required distance away for a sufficient turning allowance.
4 Adjust sleeve head by adding same amount to top of sleeve head as the difference between old shoulder length and the new, from points **a** to **b** (fig 27b), eg, if the pattern shoulder length was 10 cm and actual shoulder length is 8 cm the difference is 2 cm, which can be added to the sleeve head (between **a** and **b**). Draw in new sleeve head curve and add turnings (use extra paper stuck down). Be extra careful with low necklines, that you make these adjustments correctly.

Adjusting for wide shoulders (lengthening)

1 Place extra tissue under bodice back pattern, and front pattern, at armhole edge and stick down.
2 Measure off new shoulder length on to bodice, both sections (fig 28a).
3 Draw in new fitting line and add turning allowances. Cut on turning allowance lines (fig 28a).
4 From point **a** to **b** on top centre of sleeve, *subtract* the amount which is the difference between the old shoulder length and the new, eg, if the difference is 2 cm then subtract 2 cm from sleeve head. Draw in the new sleeve head line. Add turning allowances and cut on this line (fig 28b).

Large bust

The pattern may have to be widened and lengthened (see instructions for bodice alterations). If the waist then becomes too big, alter this as given for waist adjustments.

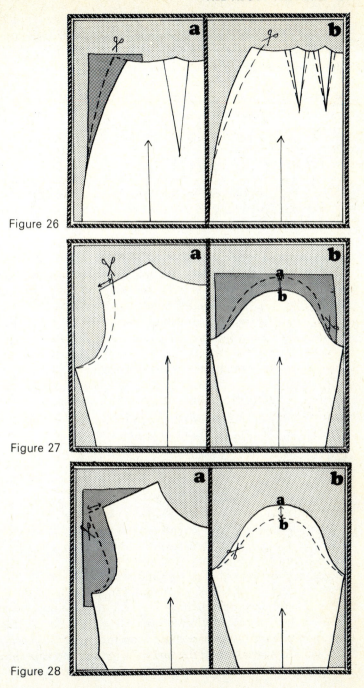

Figure 26

Figure 27

Figure 28

Small bust
The pattern may have to be made narrower and shorter (see instructions for bodice alterations). If waist becomes too small alter as for waist adjustments.

Note: Some pattern alterations can be made after the garment is cut out and tried on for fitting. If this is done, allow enough seam turnings to make any adjustments. (See chapter 10 for fitting.)

◎ METRIC CONVERSION ◎

Once you grasp that the metric system uses ones and tens as units, it becomes fairly easy to get the hang of it. The real difficulty (if any) lies in the actual conversion from the British system to the metric, before metric is assimilated into daily use. With a little commonsense (plus an ability to add and subtract accurately) we should be able to overcome the problems. To help you I have listed a table of metric conversion for lengths and sizes most often used in needlework. I've usually taken the centimetre as the standard unit, but a metre unit (100 cm) could just as easily be used by moving the decimal point two places to the left (divide by 100), eg, 1·5 cm (seam allowance) is the same as 0·015 metres.

I've also listed the figure to actually use in the column to the right of the metric measurement, as it would be too difficult for you to mark off such small amounts otherwise. However, if you do want to know what measurements to use for larger sizes (say the equivalent of $4\frac{1}{2}$ yd or $15\frac{1}{2}$ in) then don't round off the numbers until they have been added together. Use a paper and pencil if it helps. As the old British system is no longer used we will usually work to nearest cm.

Fashion design and sketching
This information has been included for those of you who are interested in fashion design but are put off through lack of drawing skill! Don't be scared if you cannot draw very well. Of course it helps if you are a budding artist, but the essential thing is to be able to give a good idea of clothes, their style and line.

Arms, legs, hands, feet, heads (all the difficult parts) don't have to be completely drawn in. It is best to accentuate any design features so that they are more noticeable. You can do this by outlining or filling in one part more than the other.

If you do want to draw the body the guides opposite should help, although these are only approximations of proportion.

Conversion tables

British Unit (inch)	Metric (centimetre)	Use	British Unit (inch)	Metric (centimetre)	Use
$\frac{1}{16}$	0·158	0·2	18 = $\frac{1}{2}$ yd	45·72	45·7
$\frac{1}{8}$	0·317	0·3	19	48·26	48·3
$\frac{1}{4}$	0·635	0·5 or 0·6	20 = $\frac{1}{2}$ metre	50·80	50·8
$\frac{1}{2}$	1·27	1·3	21	53·34	53·3
$\frac{5}{8}$ (seam			22	55·88	55·9
allowance)	1·587	1·5 or 1·6	23	58·42	58·4
$\frac{3}{4}$	1·905	1·9	24 = 2 ft ($\frac{2}{3}$ yd)	60·96	61·0
1	2·54	2·5	25	63·50	63·5
2	5·08	5·1	26	66·04	66·0
3	7·62	7·6	27 = $\frac{3}{4}$ yd	68·58	68·6
4 = $\frac{1}{10}$ metre	10·16	10·2	28	71·12	71·1
5	12·70	12·7	29	73·66	73·7
6	15·24	15·2	30 = $\frac{3}{4}$ metre	76·20	76·2
7	17·78	17·8	31	78·74	78·7
8	20·32	20·3	32	81·28	81·3
9	22·86	22·9	33	83·82	83·8
10 = $\frac{1}{4}$ metre	25·40	25·4	34	86·36	86·4
11	27·94	27·9	35	88·90	88·9
12 = 1 ft ($\frac{1}{3}$ yd)	30·48	30·5	36 = 3 ft (1 yd)	91·44	91·4
13 = $\frac{1}{3}$ metre	33·02	33·0	37	93·98	94·0
14	35·56	35·5	38	96·52	96·5
15	38·10	38·1	39	99·06	99·0
16	40·64	40·6	40 = 1 metre	101·6	101·6
17	43·18	43·2			

Average proportions
Think of the body as though it were made up of seven almost equal parts with the crotch coming just below halfway down the body.

Head and neck = one seventh
Shoulders to bust = one seventh
Bust to stomach = one seventh
Stomach to crotch = almost one seventh
Crotch to just above knee = one seventh
Knee to just below calf = one seventh
Calf to heel = one seventh.

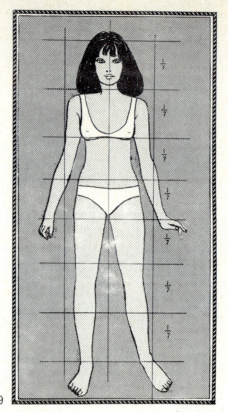

Figure 29

The width proportions are:

Centre neck to shoulder = one seventh of height
Width of waist = approx one seventh of height
Width of hips (from centre to side) = just under one seventh of height.

If you draw a pencil line where you want the figure to come on the page and mark off the top and the bottom as the height of the figure, then it is a simple matter to divide the remainder lightly into seven and using the measurement of one division as a guide, mark off the width of the figure at the shoulders, waist and hips. Filling in the figure won't be child's play, but it will be easier than it would have been without this tip (fig 29).

Adapting a pattern
You can experiment with your own designs by drawing up a few

ideas, then altering a basic pattern to incorporate them (keeping the changes simple at first). Necklines, collar shapes, sleeves, waistlines, design details, can all be adapted from a very basic pattern.

If you are designing something important it is best to make up a *toile* first (the main pattern is cut out from calico or cheap white cotton, and the parts sewn together using the largest sewing machine stitch). Draw on the toile in soft pencil, any new design lines or details. Cut down to any new fitting lines, eg, neckline, and look at the effect. Add extra pieces of fabric for collars etc and try out as many variations as you can.

Once you have decided on the design you can unpick the toile and transfer the new pattern lines to the paper pattern for cutting out (or use the toile itself as a pattern). Don't forget to leave turning allowances. It is easier to work with a toile (fig 30) because it is three-dimensional whereas a paper pattern is flat.

The illustrations in fig 31 show a few ideas for design adapting and patterns for various sleeve and collar styles etc. If you wish to alter a pattern drastically, then you should check with the library for a book which deals mainly with dress pattern design and adaptations.

Golden rules for patterns
1 Try to buy a pattern nearest your own size and figure type.

Figure 30

Figure 31

2 If you have difficulty obtaining your size, buy the next size down as all patterns give an allowance for movement. Also it is usually easier to adjust a pattern up a little than to make it smaller all over.
3 Buy dress, coat, blouse and jacket patterns by bust size; buy trouser and skirt patterns by waist size (unless hips are much bigger than pattern allows for, in which case buy by hip size).
4 If money is a problem, get a friend of the same size to share the cost of a pattern with you.
5 Try to buy a good make of pattern, as some are difficult for the beginner to use. The type with printed fitting lines and marking

are easier to follow than those which have perforations, until you get used to them.

6 Get a friend to take your measurements. It is a more accurate method than taking your own because she (or he) won't have to stretch to take them.

7 Take measurements whilst wearing a slip or bra ·and pants. Never pull the tape measure too tightly. It may save embarrassment if you are plump, but will cost money if you cut out a garment to the wrong size.

8 Note down a number of hem level measurements such as mini, midi and maxi. This will give an approximate guide when next making skirts and dresses.

9 Adjust pattern before cutting out, rather than try to alter cut fabric afterwards.

10 Keep pattern pieces not in use in their envelope.

11 Check that you have the right number of pieces out for the garment view that you want, and choose the right layout for your fabric width.

12 Never alter width amount on centre front or centre back, as this can throw the whole garment out of balance.

13 Remember that if bodice width is altered all the way down, waist and neck measurements will be altered too!

Words and terms used in this chapter (see Glossary for meanings)
Sewing terms

figure type	perforations (pattern)	turning allowance
fitting lines	straight grain	
pattern size	toile	

General terms

accommodate	drastic(ally)	metric system
accurate	entails	nape
calculation	excess	parallel
centimetre	incorporate	proportions
coincide	indication	scaled down
commercial	intimidated	three-dimensional
conversion	logical	transferred
crotch	metre	

Things to do

1 Take your own measurements (get a friend to help you) and list them in a book or on a card which you can keep. Check your

measurements against those of the standard pattern size and figure types and choose the nearest to your own.

2 List any places where alterations will have to be made on the pattern and say how you might do this.

3 Choose a basic pattern, then design new sections, such as collars. Draw a whole series of new designs.

◎ ◎ ◎

3. All About Fabrics

The range of fabrics you can use today is almost unlimited and new ones are being developed every year. Originally all fabrics were made from natural fibres (see definition below) and threads, including cotton, linen, silk and wool, but eventually scientists discovered a way of making artificial silk from cotton or wood pulp mixed with chemicals. They called this fabric *Rayon*. Then, after a period of experimentation and research, purely synthetic fibres were developed using chemicals and gases in special processes. We can now obtain a complete choice of man-made and synthetic fabrics ranging from the *Nylons* and *Terylene* through to the *Acrylics* and *Elastofibres*. To understand why certain fabrics and fibres are more suitable than others for a particular garment or article, you must know something about the properties of the fibres which make the threads that are woven into the fabrics.

Definition: A *fibre* is the smallest part of a thread; it is hair-like or even finer.

◎ VEGETABLE FIBRES ◎

Cotton

Probably one of the first materials you will use when starting needlework will be a cotton or cotton mixture of some kind. Cotton is grown in many hot countries all over the world (Egypt, Africa, America, West Indies, etc) where the cotton plants can ripen their pods in the sun. The pods burst into fluffy, white 'bolls' and these are made of the cotton linters that are collected,

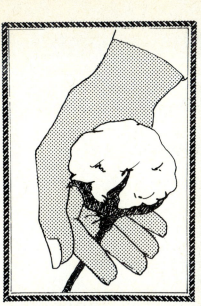

Figure 32   Figure 33

cleaned, combed, carded and processed until they are ready to be spun into thread (fig 32).

The weight and texture of the fabric may vary from the flimsiest cotton voile to the heaviest denim; from the smoothest cotton satin to the knobbly texture of towelling or the deep pile of cotton velvet. Whatever the weight or texture, if it is made of cotton it will have all the properties of cotton. For sewing, use Coats' Drima.

Properties of cotton

1 Cotton is strong and even stronger when wet. It is ideal for clothes and articles which have to take a good deal of laundering.

2 It is mothproof.

3 White cotton can be bleached to a certain degree without harming the fibres, but overbleaching causes eventual damage.

4 Cotton is cool to wear and highly absorbent. It is, therefore, a very good fabric choice for underwear, nightwear, sportswear, shirts and all clothes which are worn close to the body.

5 Cotton may be susceptible to mildew and bacteria, so keep out of damp conditions.

6 It may shrink if not pre-treated.

Mixtures such as wool/cotton or cotton/*Terylene* usually bring together the good qualities of each fibre.

Linen

Linen is made from the flax plant (fig 33) which is grown in Ireland, Belgium and France. The linen itself comes from the fibre bundles found in the stalk of the flax plant when ripe. When the gummy substances holding them together are removed, the bundles are separated and processed, then spun into thread. Use Coats' Drima.

Properties of linen
1 It is very strong (stronger than cotton), even when wet.
2 It is very cool and absorbent.
3 It is mothproof but susceptible to rot due to bacteria or acids.
4 It can be gently bleached (whites only).
5 It may crease easily unless treated with a special finish.
6 It may shrink if not pre-treated.
7 Linen can be used for all the purposes that cotton can and it is finer and usually wears better. It is more costly to produce than cotton and is generally more expensive.

◎ MAN-MADE CELLULOSE FIBRES ◎ (Vegetable Fibres)

Rayons
Viscose rayon
This is a regenerated vegetable fibre made by treating wood pulp (usually from spruce pine trees) with chemicals and using a special process (fig 34). The liquid is forced through tubes to form jets

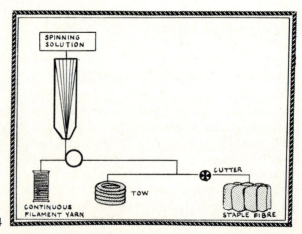

Figure 34

which harden into filaments, which the fibres can be made from. Some of the trade names of viscose rayon are as follows: *Evlan, Vincel, Sarille, Durafil*, etc.

Properties of viscose rayon
1 Mothproof, but can be susceptible to bacteria when damp.
2 Exposure to acid can cause rotting.
3 Absorbs moisture and is fairly cool to wear.
4 Soft to the touch and so will drape well.
5 Not very strong or hard-wearing, therefore not suitable for garments which need a lot of laundering. (*Vincel* is an improved and stronger type of rayon. *Evlan* is much stronger and is used in carpets etc.)
6 Melts at high temperature so needs careful ironing.
7 May shrink slightly unless pre-treated.
  Blends or mixtures of rayon usually incorporate the properties of the other fibre(s).

Sewing: Has a tendency to fray so cut wider seam turnings. Use Coats' Drima.

Diacetate rayon
This was the original 'Artificial Silk' and was made from cotton linters or wood pulp and chemicals using a similar process to that of viscose rayon. Trade names include *Dicel, Lansil, Lansofil, Lo-Flam-Dicel* and *Lancolene*.

Properties of diacetate rayon
1 Absorbent and fairly cool.
2 Soft and silky to touch. Drapes well.
3 Mothproof but attacked by bacteria and mildew when damp.
4 Not especially hard-wearing except for some treated acetates, eg, *Dicel*, which is a stronger type, both colourfast and washable.
5 Very hot water can soften fibres and strong acids or alkalis can damage them.
6 The fibres melt at high temperatures and so need careful ironing.

Sewing: Use very fine needles and pins for hand sewing to avoid markings. Use Coats' Drima.

Triacetate rayon
Made in a similar way to diacetate rayon; the components are the same but the production process is slightly different It is much stronger than diacetate. Trade names are: *Tricel, Tricelon*.

Properties of triacetate rayon
1 Stronger than other rayons but not as strong as *Nylon* or *Terylene*.
2 Mothproof but attacked by bacteria when damp.
3 Softens at a much higher temperature than other rayons but still needs care with heat, eg, ironing.
4 Can be treated with special finishes to produce crease resistance and permanent pleating.
5 Repels water and dries quickly.
6 Needs little ironing.
7 Stain resistant.
8 Soft to the touch.
9 Not as absorbent as viscose rayons or natural vegetable fibres.
10 Holds its shape and size better than any other rayon type.
    (Triacetate rayon is often blended with wool, cotton, etc, to make them washable or easier to dry.)

Sewing: As for diacetates.

◎ ANIMAL FIBRES (Protein Fibres) ◎

Wool
Wool comes from the hair or fur of animals (fig 35) such as sheep, rabbits, camels, llamas, goats and even the Tibetan yak! It can be made into varying textures, weights and finishes after spinning and dyeing, and can be knitted or woven into fabrics. The best quality wools are Merino and Vicuna.

Properties of wool
1 Wool is only one third as strong as cotton.
2 The fibres will stretch to 3 or 4 times their own length, having high stretchability (returning almost to the same length). Because they are so highly elastic, they regain their original shape after washing (if washed with care).
3 Highly resilient and therefore crease resistant.
4 Very absorbent and after absorbing moisture becomes warm. This makes it good for winter clothes.
5 Wool fibres have scales and if they are incorrectly washed or rubbed, these scales interlock causing 'felting' which makes the wool look unattractive and shrink. To avoid this, rub wool as little as possible when washing. Some wool mixtures do not have this problem.

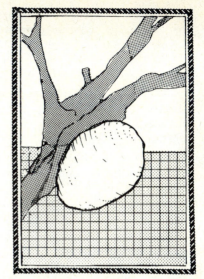

Figure 35   Figure 36

6 Wool chars at high temperatures so needs some care when ironing.

7 Attacked by moth unless treated.

8 Attacked by bacteria under damp conditions.

9 Warm because a poor conductor of heat, the scales in the fibres trapping air in pockets which hold the warmth in.

10 Harmed by some bleaches such as chlorine, but not weak hydrogen peroxide.

Silk

Silk was first used in China about 5000 years ago and has been one of the most valued of textile fibres. It is obtained from the cocoon of the silk worm (fig 36). This little insect makes itself a casing of a gummy substance spun from openings on its head. The substance (seracin) hardens on contact with the air and is made into a cocoon which protects the pupa while it is going through the stages of metamorphosis (eventually emerging as a moth). The processes used for man-made fibres are really just a sophisticated adaptation of the natural processes of the silk worm (extruding liquid fibre through spinnerets is the same as pushing liquid substances through holes – see further on).

Silk thread is obtained by unravelling the cocoons and washing away the gummy parts of the fibres. The fibres are then spun into threads. Because most of the process for reeling the threads is done by hand, silk remains one of the more expensive fabrics. For sewing, use Coats' Drima.

Properties of silk
1 Not liable to attack by moths because fibres do not contain sulphur which attracts them.
2 Harmed by some bleaches such as chlorine, but not weak hydrogen peroxide.
3 Easily dyed.
4 Has a natural resilience and is therefore crease resistant to a degree.
5 Some types are easy to launder but others must be dry cleaned.
6 Is a bad conductor of heat and therefore can be very warm whilst being light in weight (mountaineers wear silk gloves under their mittens for extra warmth).

◎ SYNTHETICS: ◎
The Other Man-mades

Although rayons are man-made they are not purely synthetic. Synthetics are man-made fibres which have no natural vegetable or animal substance. They are mostly made from carbon-based compounds artificially processed, eg, coal, petroleum, etc.

There are three main types of synthetic fibre which you will encounter in needlework (there are others but you will be less likely to be using fabrics made from these fibres).

1 The polyamide group: *Nylon, Celon, Enkalon, Bri-Nylon*, etc.
2 The polyester group: *Terylene* (including *Crimplene*), *Dacron, Trevira, Terlenka, Teteron*, etc.
3 The acrylics: *Acrilan, Orlon, Courtelle, Dralon*, etc.

The names listed above are mostly trade names for one or other of the groups and each fibre is made by a similar process. This involves different chemical and mineral substances plus air and water, sprayed through nozzled jets called spinnerets (they do actually spin round) and the liquids harden on contact with air. They may be washed or rinsed in other chemicals before being spun into continuous threads or chopped up into staple fibres (short threads which can be crimped or processed to form wool-like fibre).

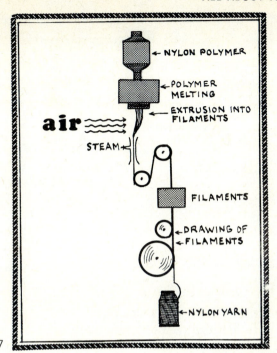

Figure 37

Polyamides
Nylon

This was the first of the synthetics and was discovered in 1937. It is made from chemicals, coal, air and water. It can be made into *staple yarn*, small lengths, or *continuous filament yarn*, one long length (see fig 37).

Properties of nylon

1 Has a high resistance to wear, and is therefore very good mixed with weaker fibres, eg, wool, to give them strength and a long life.
2 Makes its own static electricity and may attract dirt more than natural fibres do.
3 Does not stretch or shrink so retains shape after washing.
4 Is a bad conductor of heat and therefore very warm to wear.
5 Has a low absorbency which makes it easy to wash and dry. It can be clammy to wear in hot weather as some weaves do not allow the skin to 'breathe' by letting the perspiration through.
6 Melts at high temperatures, therefore needs careful ironing. Care in washing is also necessary to avoid permanent creasing.

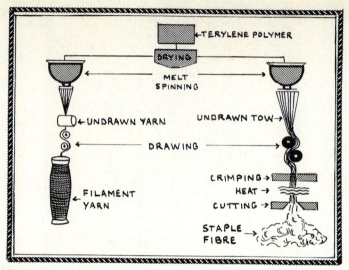

Figure 38

7 Not attacked by moth; rot resistant.
8 Can discolour with age (especially white Nylons).

Sewing: Loosen upper tension to avoid puckering. If necessary, place tissue paper between presser foot and fabric. Use French or enclosed seams (see chapter 12) with Coats' Drima.

Polyesters
Terylene
First discovered in 1941, this synthetic fibre is one of the most important. Made from chemicals obtained from petroleum; when the processing has produced the polyester it hardens and is cut into small chips; the chips are melted and this solution is forced through spinnerets to make the yarn (fig 38).

Properties of polyesters (Terylene)
1 Has a very low absorbency (therefore difficult to dye, but very quick to wash and dry).
2 Is a bad conductor of heat and therefore warm to wear. It is clammy to wear in hot weather unless mixed with a natural fibre such as cotton.
3 Has a good resistance to heat and so has a higher melting point than most synthetics.
4 May shrink slightly unless pre-treated.

5 Does not stretch, therefore retains its shape well. Has no elasticity so is no good for tights or stockings.
6 Not attacked by moth; rot resistant.
7 White Terylene is less likely to discolour than many synthetics but will yellow slightly with age or the wrong washing treatment.

Sewing: As for Nylon.

Crimplene
This is a polyester of the same type as Terylene but slightly changed in that it has a low stretch and is used to make a high bulk yarn.

Properties of Crimplene
As for Terylene but with the addition of a low stretch making it suitable for knitwear.

Acrylics
The trade names for the acrylics include *Acrilan, Orlon, Courtelle, Dralon*, etc. Each is made in a similar way to the other synthetics but involving different chemicals.

Acrilan: Made from air and natural gas.
Orlon: Made from coal, limestone, air and water.
Courtelle: Made from petrol, air and water.

Properties of the acrylics
1 Warm and soft to the touch, therefore nearest to wool fibres.
2 Good shape retention because they do not stretch (except certain kinds of knitwear which need special care when washing).
3 Dry quicker than wool and are harder wearing.
4 Moth and rot resistant.
5 White acrylics are likely to discolour with age.

Sewing: Loosen top tension to avoid stretching (see chapter 4, under sewing machines). Use Coats' Drima.

As well as the previous three kinds of synthetic fibre there are others, eg, the modacrylics such as *Teklan* and *Dynel* (which are flame resistant), and the elastofibres made of polyurethane such as *Spanzelle* and *Lycra* (which have good elasticity) used in underwear, swimwear and foundation garments. These fibres are rot resistant to perspiration.

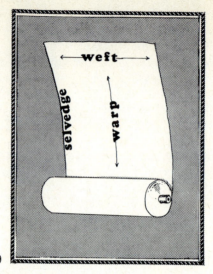

Figure 39

Yarns and weaves

Definition: Yarn consists of fibres twisted together to form a length which is strong enough to be knitted or woven into a fabric.

When fibres are made they are then spun into twisted threads called yarns. These can be of varying thicknesses, textures and lengths, according to the fibres used and the fabric to be made. When the yarns are woven together they make a weave, and this weave can vary according to how the threads are woven.

There are two ways for the threads to go when making a fabric. The *warp* threads are those which run up and down the fabric in a vertical line following the line of the selvedge (the firm edge at each side of the fabric). These are the first to be threaded on the loom. The *weft* threads are those which are threaded in and out of the warp threads and give the fabric its pattern or weave. According to how these horizontal weft threads are woven, the weave of the fabric will be decided (fig 39).

Some weaves follow the straight grain (ie, the straight lines made by the warp and weft threads being at right angles to each other) and some will look as if they follow the true cross (at a 45° angle to the straight grain). *Twill weaves* such as denim, appear as though they are following a true cross, but if you look very carefully you will see that the threads are woven in a straight line. Certain threads are missed out on each line which gives this crossway or diagonal effect (fig 40).

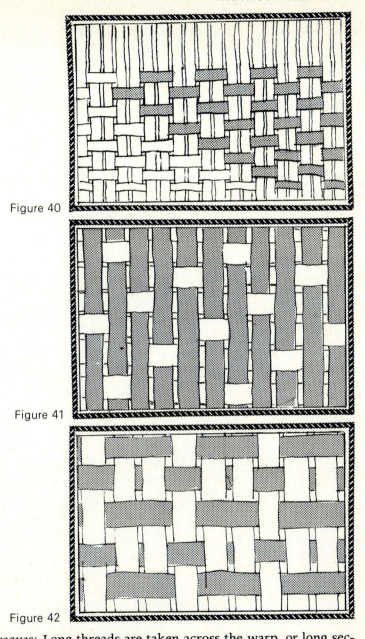

Figure 40

Figure 41

Figure 42

Satin weaves: Long threads are taken across the warp, or long sections of warp thread left exposed making a slub, giving a smooth satin-like finish (fig 41).

Haircord weaves: These have a basket-like weave. The weft threads are taken across two warp threads and under one warp thread, alternating on different rows (fig 42).

Herringbone weaves: These are woven in a pattern following the shape of herringbone stitch, starting diagonally in one direction but dipping down to the other, alternating across the row to give the distinctive look of the weave (fig 43).

Basket or hopsack weave: Weft threads are taken across two warp threads and under two warp threads. This is repeated for two rows then alternated for two rows, giving a basket-like appearance (fig 44).

Plain weave: Normal weave for most cotton lawns etc. Each weft thread goes under and over one warp thread, and alternates on the

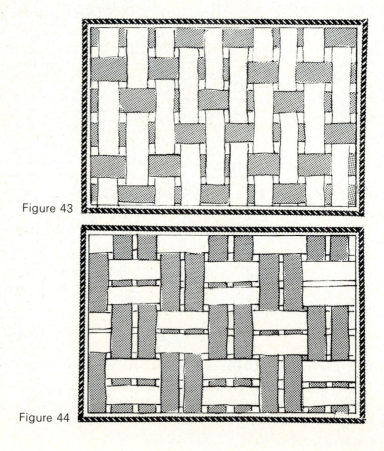

Figure 43

Figure 44

following row. It is a very strong weave because the threads are closely packed together (fig 45).

Pile weave: Extra threads are woven into threads of a plain weave backing, making loops which can be cut to give a soft pile, as in velvet, or left as they are as in towelling (fig 46).

◎ WORKING WITH SPECIAL FABRICS ◎

Some fabrics sold commercially require special handling when making up. Some of these types and how to work with them are listed alphabetically as follows.

Diagonal weaves and patterns
Definition: Any fabric which has the weave or pattern at an angle

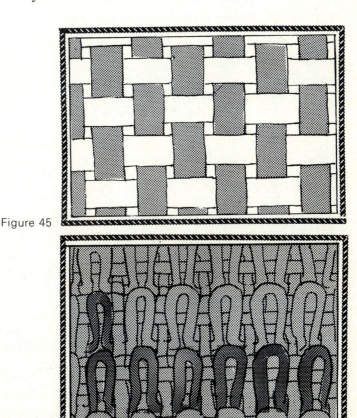

Figure 45

Figure 46

from the straight grain, eg, twill weave denims, gaberdine, wool tweed and flannel.

Pattern or weave should be matched up on these fabrics as this may make a difference to the look or colour effect of the finished garment. Never use obvious diagonals where there is going to be difficulty matching them, in flared panelled skirts, magyar type sleeves, etc. Use for designs which do not have a great deal of seam joining or matching. Extra care is needed with collars, pockets and design details.

Cutting
Reverse pattern pieces and the material where there is a right and a left side. This gives a chevron effect which is only possible with reversible fabric (fig 47b). For diagonals running in one direction only, cut one piece first and move pattern across and reverse it; all diagonals will be going the same way (fig 47a).

Fur fabrics and imitation pelts
These fabrics can range from real skins (treat very carefully indeed, as minks are hard to come by!) to the fake nylon 'funfurs'. In every case a little care in cutting will ensure success (fig 48).

Cutting
Treat as one-way fabric (see page 56). Lay pattern tops all pointing same way. Hairs or fur should go in same direction. Cut long-haired fur so that hairs run *down* the garment. If fabric is weighty or thick

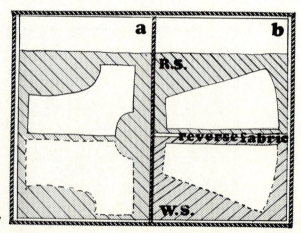

Figure 47

Figure 48

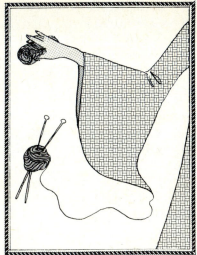

Figure 49

use a razor blade or sharp knife instead of scissors (for easier cutting
– but be careful). Avoid cutting through hairs as this gives a sharp
unnatural edge. For pressing, see chapter 24.

Knitted fabrics

These range from knobbly tweed wools to smooth tricot jerseys.
They should all be treated the same when cutting. The straight
grain is usually the lengthways rib of the knit. Material should be
folded along the line of rib in the centre. Pin or tack fabric to prevent
slippage whilst cutting. Press out folds of tubular fabrics as these
are not always on the straight grain. If edges of a knitted fabric start
to curl up, pin flat down together (fig 49).

Sewing

Use ballpoint needle, small to medium stitches; always stay stitch
curved edges (see chapter 6). Where possible make a separate lining
for the fabric or back it with an interlining made up in one with the
fabric, giving a bonded look. Never use a double hem edge – a
single tailor's hem is best (see chapter 23). Use seam binding on
seams and waistlines and some armholes (see chapter 20). If seam
edges curl up, catch stitch them to the main part of garment with
small stitches invisible from right side.

Laminated fabrics (eg, PVC)

These are coated with a plastic surface of some kind over a fibre or foam backing. These fabrics do not usually need lining, as the plastic coating prevents creases and gives extra 'body' (fig 50).

Cutting

It is easier to lay pattern on wrong side of fabric (less likely to slip). Stick pattern in place with sticky tape outside the seam allowance and cut round. Mark darts etc with tailor's chalk on wrong side (see chapter 5, Marking). Before sewing, fix seams etc together with sticky tape or paper clips along the length, removing as you reach it, or stick two pieces together with fabric glue following the seam allowance. Sometimes this may hold the seam together without stitching.

Sewing

Coat presser foot with talc or flour if sewing on the shiny side, or use a Nylon foot especially made for the purpose, if your machine will take it, or use a silicone spray. For foam-back fabrics place a layer of tissue *underneath* and also *above* the seam to enable the fabric to move freely. Use a medium-sized needle and set stitch length to largest size to avoid making too many holes in fabric. Stick down hems and facing with fabric glue. Do not iron unless absolutely necessary (use a cool iron on wrong side; never iron foam-backs).

Napped fabrics

Definition: Any fabric which has a hairy or downy surface which can be left unbrushed or brushed in one direction.

These materials include everything from wool flannel to brushed denim, from fleece to suede skin. Sometimes if the word 'nap' is mentioned, it refers to any fabric which has a 'one-way' pattern, as the cutting and layout process is the same for both.

One-way fabrics

Definition: One which has its design moving in one direction only, eg, a print of flowers all standing up the same way.

As well as napped fabrics which have a surface depth, there are also 'pile' fabrics. These too have a surface depth, but it is usually greater.

Figure 50

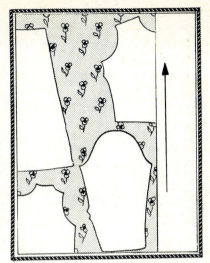

Figure 51

Pile fabrics

Definition: A piled fabric is one which has loops or tufts woven into the design giving a raised and often uneven surface depth.

Because all these types of fabrics must be cut in a special way, more fabric will be needed than allowed for in the pattern for normal fabric. Check amount of fabric given on pattern for naps, piles, and one-way designs. If the pattern does not include this information then an extra $\frac{1}{2}-\frac{3}{4}$ metre will be necessary, perhaps more for large patterns.

Cutting
The way that nap or pile fabrics are cut will alter their appearance. A nap or pile going upwards makes the fabric appear darker, a nap or pile going downwards makes the fabric appear lighter. A useful guide is to cut nap fabrics (mostly woollens) going downwards and pile fabrics (velvets etc) going upwards. To tell which way nap is running, stroke fingers up and down it – when nap is running downwards it will feel smooth to the touch.

After choosing which way nap or pile is to run, lay all pattern pieces so top of each piece lies in same direction. Any one-way patterns should have tops placed to top of fabric, eg, flowers growing upwards (fig 51).

Sewing
1 Always tack seams together.
2 Lessen pressure of presser foot for naps and piles and use a longer stitch than usual.
3 Don't top stitch directly on pile or nap fabrics – this causes flattening. Place a layer of tissue paper between fabric and presser foot and remove after stitching. (For pressing velvets etc, see chapter 24.)

Plaids and checks
From $\frac{1}{2}$–1 metre extra fabric is needed for matching plaids.

Cutting
Fold material along length if *two* layers of pattern are to be cut and pin fabric along lines of plaid both ways to prevent slippage.

Cut pattern as for one-way fabric. Try to get plaids matched at side seams, shoulders, top of sleeves, etc. Keep grain lines straight and try to match at armhole area also (fig 52). Uneven plaids may need special care in balancing the pattern. It is best to cut these types through one thickness only. Adjust adjoining section accordingly (to match the first). For plaid chevrons fabric must be the same both sides (ie, not having a noticeable right and wrong side). Pieces are then cut in reverse so they can be matched.

Sewing
Use slip basting stitch or slip hemming to hold sections together, so matching the pattern correctly (see chapter 7, Hand Stitches).

Sheer fabrics
These include fine wool voile, nylon, silk chiffon, etc. When cutting, snip selvedge every so often if used in seams, to prevent puckering.

Sewing
1 Use bindings rather than facings for neatening edges (see chapter 20, Bindings).
2 Use French seams on special garments, eg, evening blouse, or Quick French seams, cut narrow, on garments which are not so important, eg, underwear (see chapter 12, Seams).
3 Cut hems exactly double the width of finished hem, ie, first and second hem turnings are the same depth. It looks neater and more decorative to have the hem finished this way.

Slippery fabrics
Many fabrics such as Nylon jersey will slip away from you as you

Figure 52

Figure 53

are handling or sewing them (fig 53). To avoid this a few simple precautions are necessary:

1 Pin selvedges and crossway ends together. Working along length of fabric, pin through all layers at regular intervals.

2 Stick edges of fabric to cutting table with sticky tape to prevent it slipping.

3 Use tissue paper between fabric and presser foot when sewing. Remove later.

Stretch fabrics

Some patterns are for stretch fabrics only. For dresses, skirts or jackets the stretch should be across the fabric so the 'give' is around the body (fig 54).

Cutting

Don't let stretch fabric hang over edge of cutting table (this can cause excessive stretching). Lay pattern pieces as for one-way (so each piece stretches in same direction – except parts which are to stretch in a different direction). Put pins about 5 cm apart. Don't stretch fabric when cutting. Keep as flat as possible. Use very sharp scissors to avoid tugging material.

Sewing

Use zig-zag stitch or special stretch stitch if machine does it. If

Figure 54

lining stretch fabric use a lining which also has some stretch to it, eg, tricot knit. Don't attach lining to seams or hems (to avoid pulling). Make up separately and attach at shoulder. Interface areas which should not stretch, eg, buttonholes, necklines. (For pressing, see chapter 24.)

Words and terms used in this chapter (see Glossary for meanings)
Sewing terms

acrylics	lustre	slub (bed)
bolls	nap	spinnerets
carded	pile	staple fibres
cellulosic fibres	plaid	synthetics
continuous	polyamides	tension
(filament yarns)	polyesters	tricot
cotton linters	polyurethanes	true cross
felting	regenerated fibres	warp
fibres	retention	weave
interface	resilient	weft
laminated	selvedge	zig-zag

General terms

absorbent	cocoon	distinctive
artificial	components	fibrous
bacteria	diagonal	horizontal

imitation	mineral	static electricity
incorporate	properties	susceptible
metamorphosis	pupa	vertical
mildew	resistant	

Things to do
1 Work out a basic wardrobe for a working girl, giving choice of fabric and reasons for choice.
2 Collect together as many pieces of fabric (scraps) as you can and stick them in a book listing their names; what fibres you think they are made of, what properties they have and so on.
3 Collect together scraps of unusual fabrics, eg, those with a pile, lace, etc. Machine on these, testing tension and so on, making a note of stitches used and any special methods. Mount them with the notes in a scrap-book.

◎   ◎   ◎

4. Worker's Choice

A sound knowledge of the tools of the trade is an essential starting point for the needlework beginner. This means knowing how to look after them as well as how to use them correctly.

The most expensive equipment is not always the best and not always necessary, but try to have the best *you* can afford, starting with the basic tools (fig 55). If you take good care of them they will last a lifetime. If you have to borrow or share equipment, take as much care of it as you would of your own.

◎ SEWING MACHINES ◎

Before sewing machines were invented people would sew their clothes together using a variety of hand stitches. Today, with all the modern aids, a lot of handwork is no longer necessary. There are so many makes and kinds of sewing machine about now, which take the hard work from needlework, but because there are so many types the following information is of a general nature only. Always check with the instruction manual of the machine you are using if you are in any doubt at all.

Figure 55

There are three major types of sewing machine:

1 *Treadle*: Worked by pushing a plate up and down with the feet; this guides a belt that turns the wheel. Straight stitches usually.

2 *Hand machines*: These have a wheel at the side with a manually turned handle. Straight stitches only.

3 *Electric machines*: These are run by an electric motor usually guided by the foot on a kind of accelerator. Can be straight stitch or swing needle.

The variations of electric machines can be divided into:

A *Straight stitch*
These sew only straight stitches. Suitable for all straight stitching, attaching shirring elastic, some types of edge finishing (see chapter 18, Seam Finishes) and straight stitch embroidery (use coloured thread and follow traced pattern).

B *Swing needle*
These have a stitch width regulator which causes the needle to swing from side to side in a variety of widths.

The two kinds of swing needle are:

1 **Semi-automatics**: These sew straight stitch, satin stitch, also zig-zag. Can do basic stitching, oversew edges, make buttonholes and do appliqué. Some will do stretch stitch (for jersey fabrics etc) and some will do a few decorative stitches.

2 **Fully automatics**: These do all that the other machines do, plus an extra selection of fancy stitches for machine embroidery. Either the addition of discs changes the programme of machine patterns, or this can be done by altering certain dial selectors. The dials you are likely to find on machines (but not necessarily located in same place as on fig 56) are:

a *Stitch length dial*: From zero setting upwards. Often the smaller the number the smaller the stitch, eg, stitch length 1 is a *short* stitch; stitch length 4 is a *long* stitch (suitable for gathering or vinyl fabrics etc. See also page 66).

b *Stitch width dial*: From zero upwards. Set to zero will give a straight stitch.

c *Stitch selector dial*: This tells what stitch machine is programmed for, eg, zig-zag, blindhemming, etc; must be changed when stitch type is changed.

There may also be a control to change needle position; usually

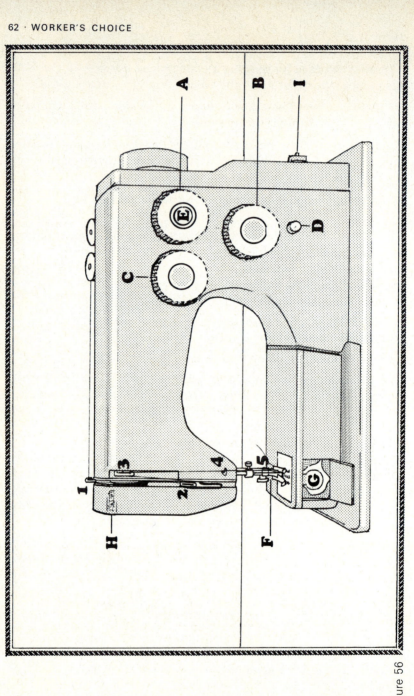

Figure 56

kept centralized, this can be moved to right or left for making buttonholes etc.

d *Drop feed*: A small button or lever which lowers feed dog plate (metal teeth which feed material through). Useful for free embroidery, machine darning, or to make placing of thick materials under the presser foot an easier job. In latter case put feed dog plate back up before machining.

e *Reverse button*: Usually located near the stitch size regulators. Causes machine to work backwards. Reverse can also be made by adjusting stitch length lever on some types of machine. Used for buttonholes and for securing ends of machining. Reverse stitches in a line of machining will give an 'elastic' stitch suitable for stretch fabrics if machine does not do a stretch stitch automatically (fig 57). Use for short lengths only, eg, armholes.

f *Presser foot*: (fig 58). This holds material down on to plate. Can be loosened or tightened according to the thickness of fabric.

The actual foot part can be changed and there are special presser feet made for buttonholes, embroidery and satin stitches, piping and binding, putting in zips, etc. Sometimes the whole of presser foot must be changed (by loosening off a screw at side). Sometimes

Figure 57

Figure 58

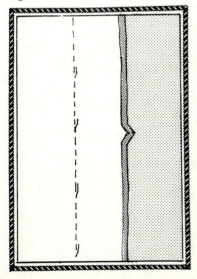

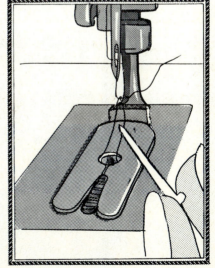

only the foot plate itself need be changed and this can be removed by unclipping.

g *Bobbin or spool*: Found in arm or bed of machine underneath needle plate. Tension of bobbin doesn't often need changing but if it does, loosen off or tighten small screw located at side of bobbin case. Only if bobbin thread (underneath thread of row of machining) looks tight when top tension is set to neutral (fig 59), should bobbin tension be changed. See chapter 6 for more information on stitches and tension.

h *Tension control*: In addition to bobbin tension control, there is another knob, dial or lever which adjusts tension or tightness of top thread (that coming from needle). It is usually this tension control which needs adjusting. On most machines a mark on the dial shows normal or neutral setting, and a movement either side of this tightens or loosens off top thread. Set the dial to neutral when practising on fabric or new stitch.

i *Bobbin winder*: Bobbins should be evenly wound only as far as outer perimeter of spool. Any thicker, excess thread may cause machine to jam.

Knobs or dials which need adjusting to wind new bobbin will vary from machine to machine but are usually located near wheel of machine. Check with instruction manual of your machine.

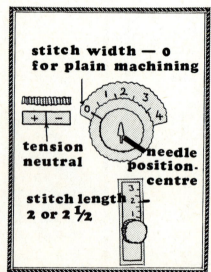

Figure 59

Using a machine

1 Wind bobbin thread and place in case.

2 Make sure thread is correctly pulled through slot in bobbin case.

3 Place bobbin in case correctly – with thread going in right direction (usually clockwise).

4 Check bobbin thread is pulling from case easily without being too loose or too tight.

5 Place bobbin case in machine. Listen or feel for click when it slots into place properly.

6 Thread up machine. Check with instruction manual as machines vary (if machine jams or fails to work properly it is often because machine or bobbin is not threaded correctly!).

7 Needles are usually threaded from right to left or from front to back (follow groove of needle to see). Check needle is not blunt, bent, broken or loose. This could cause unevenness in stitching and missed stitches (use ballpoint needle on knitteds and some synthetics to prevent this).

8 Pull up bobbin thread through needle plate by holding needle thread taut towards you and turning wheel once by hand slowly towards you, until it catches bobbin thread. Pull loop up with a pin and take both threads to back of machine (fig 58).

9 Check that all dials are set correctly before working.

10 *Most important*: when you start to machine always hold the two threads back from work and work first few stitches *turning wheel by hand whilst still holding these threads*. This avoids the 'bird's nest' type tangle in the bobbin case.

11 Practise stitch and tension on a spare piece of fabric *every time* you begin to machine or when you change a stitch type. You won't have to unpick if you make mistakes on scrap fabric.

12 When sharing a machine which is swing needle, make a note of the stitch width, length, etc, you are using. Stitches can then be repeated next time you use the machine, even if someone else has used it since.

13 Check dials at beginning and set them back to neutral when you finish (ie, stitch length $2-2\frac{1}{2}$, stitch width 0-straight stitch) especially when sharing a machine. Try to think of the machine as if it were a car with gears; put them into neutral when you stop (fig 59).

14 When machining angles or corners, always leave needle in work and lift presser foot before turning fabric. This prevents loop in machine line.

15 Use correct thread and needle for fabric and machine being used.

Scissors

A good pair of cutting-out shears (scissors with long blades) is a must for all dressmakers, and they should be kept sharp. Smaller trimming scissors are useful for trimming seams, edges, etc; embroidery scissors and paper-cutting scissors (rounded end) are also useful.

You can also buy a small tool called a stitch ripper for undoing machine stitches. It is a very quick method of undoing mistakes but quicker still is not to make any!

Tape measures, markers, etc

Fibre glass tape measures are best because they don't stretch. Wooden rules, eg, a metre stick, are handy for drawing straight lines etc. Hem gauges and tuck markers have marks or notches at a particular measurement, eg, 1·5 cm. They are used for measuring off turnings or folds evenly along a length.

Tailor's chalk, tracing paper and wheels, etc

Used for marking fabrics at balance points or on darts etc. Whatever method you use for marking it should be clear and removable by washing, or not show from right side of work. Tailor's chalk is fine for marking straight lines and some thicker fabrics. Tracing paper and wheels are also useful. The paper has a coloured, slightly waxy surface and is used with a tool which has a handle and a serrated or spoked wheel. Light coloured paper is used to mark dark fabrics, and dark paper for light fabrics (see chapter 5, under Marking).

Needles

Machine needles vary for the kind of job they must do. Many machines used now are foreign so will use the Continental size needles. The finer the weight of fabric, the *smaller* the needle number and the *shorter* the stitch *size*; the heavier the weight of fabric, the *larger* the needle number and the *longer* the stitch size. See also stitch length dial, page 61. Hand sewing needles vary from the largest darning needle to the thinnest beading needle.

Thimbles

These can be made of various materials: plastic, bone, metal, porcelain, etc. Some very beautiful, old thimbles were made of precious metals such as gold, and the daintiest one I have ever seen, at Brighton Museum, was enclosed (complete with a pair of tiny scissors and a tape measure) in a hinged-lid walnut shell. A metal thimble is really better than plastic and should fit the index (middle) finger of the right hand comfortably (left hand for the for the left-handed!).

Haberdashery (fig 60)
Sewing threads
Using the right threads for the work is very important to avoid split seams. *For handwork*, use Coats' Drima for most hand and machine sewing or Coats' Satinised no. 40. Use Clark's Anchor button thread or Coats' Bold Stitch for hand-sewn buttonholes, sewing on buttons or anywhere an especially strong thread is needed. Use tacking cotton or matt soft thread for all temporary hand stitching. *For machine work*, use Clark's Anchor machine embroidery thread for decorative stitching and Coats' Drima for all other machine sewing (on natural and synthetic fabrics of all weights).

Bindings, cords, tapes, etc
Bias binding: Comes in various widths, colours and fabrics. Crossway bindings can be made up from scraps (see chapters 8 and 20).

Paris binding, and straight or seam binding is used for neatening. edges (see chapter 18) and for making hanging loops on garments (see chapter 25).

Cotton or linen tape: Used for loops, ties, strengthening seams and openings, etc.

Petersham: A ribbed type ribbon, used at waistlines, comes in various widths, straight or shaped to a curve. Some kinds are stiffened with bone (see chapter 22).

Belt stiffening: Various widths and stiffnesses. Buy by the metre. Some kinds do not wash well so check first.

Piping cords: Various sizes and colours. Used for seams and edges etc. (See chapter 21.)

Ribbons and braids: Good selection found in most large stores. Check counters selling lampshade trimmings etc for best choice.

Interfacings: Come in two main types.
1 Woven, eg, canvas, linen, muslin, calico, horsehair, etc, in various weights and widths.

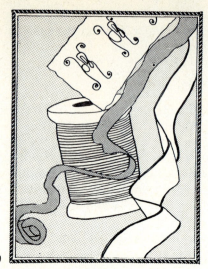

Figure 60

2 Non-woven, eg, Vilene. Comes in iron-on and plain, in various weights and qualities.

If you need more information on interfacings and interlinings, see chapter 9.

Pressing equipment: See chapter 24.

Golden rules for equipment
1 Be sure you have the right equipment for the job.
2 It should be in good working order when you start, eg, scissors should be sharp, machines oiled and so on.
3 Dust and clean equipment often.
4 Put away all tools and equipment in cases or boxes where they can be found easily and won't get damaged.

Words and terms used in this chapter (see Glossary for meanings)
Sewing terms

appliqué	instruction manual	swing needle
blindhemming	shirring	tension
bobbin	straight stitch	zig-zag

General terms

accelerator	located	puckering
adjust	manually	regulator
centralized	neutral	taut
clockwise	parallel	variations
excess	perimeter	

Things to do
1 Make a list of all the equipment you think you will need to make a dress.
2 Work out a pattern for machine embroidery using straight stitch only.
3 Without looking, list main parts of a sewing machine and give a brief description of what each part does.

PART TWO

Preparation Makes Perfect

5. Now You Can Start

The following information lists some sewing terms which you will need to know. Some of these terms you may already be familiar with, but try to remember *all* of them as they are important in needlework (fig 61).

Straight grain: Grain line or weave of fabric which is parallel to selvedge, the threads of which are known as the warp threads (the straight grain can also follow the weft threads).

Selvedge: The firm edge of fabric at each side, as it comes off the bale.

Warp: This is parallel to selvedge and running in same direction.

Weft: This is at right angles to warp threads and selvedge; it can be used as straight grain (facings etc).

True cross: This is at a 45° angle from straight grain (half a right angle).

Figure 61

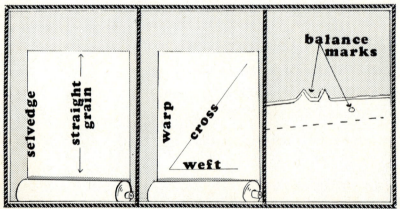

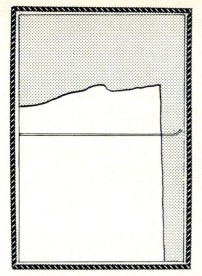

Figure 62

Figure 63

Balance marks: Any marks on pattern which should be transferred to fabric. Each section of garment is matched to its corresponding piece by aligning (matching up) these marks.

Preparing the fabric

Before cutting out a pattern it is essential to prepare the fabric, especially if it has twisted off the straight grain or is not pre-shrunk.

Straightening

Because a twisted grain can ruin the hang of a garment, straighten first by one of these methods.

1 Cut across ends of weft line or pull weft thread at each end, if this is possible. Trim fabric to this line (fig 62).

2 Clip cloth at one end and tear across, if it will tear without damaging; some fabrics such as cords and towelling will not tear accurately, so test first.

3 Lay fabric on a table, with selvedge to edge of table. Check that ends are parallel to ends of table. If they are not, stretch fabric carefully on bias or true cross, moving and pulling with both hands along selvedge for the entire length until ends are both at right angles to selvedge. The pattern (if there is one) should match when folded over. If fabric is still slightly crooked, roll in a damp cloth, leave for a while and stretch into shape.

Shrinking

If the fabric is not marked as 'pre-shrunk' it is best to shrink it before cutting (fig 63). Some fabrics unless pre-shrunk, may lose up to 7 cm in the metre. If the material is washable, wash first before cutting out pattern or use the following method which is suitable for woollens etc.

1 Wet a strip of sheeting or white cotton the length and width of the fabric to be shrunk. Remove excess moisture by wringing out, place sheeting on top of fabric to be shrunk.

2 Roll fabric up carefully with sheeting inside. Leave it for about 2–4 hours, or overnight if this is more practical. Remove sheeting and press fabric with a hot iron (over a dry pressing cloth) on wrong side of fabric. (See chapter 24, Pressing.)

Laying the pattern out

1 Before laying out pattern, original fold in centre of fabric should be pressed out. Any creases in paper pattern should also be pressed out to prevent loss of length and width in pattern.

2 Check you have right amount of fabric for view chosen and for width of fabric used and size required (fig 64).

3 Remove all pattern pieces.

4 Check you have pattern layout instruction sheet for view required and width of fabric you are using.

5 Remove all pattern pieces for that view and layout and put remaining pieces back in envelope to prevent loss.

6 Check which pieces are to be cut double, single, or placed to a fold.

7 If material has one-way design, pile or nap, check layout for this (see chapter 3).

8 Lay main pattern pieces on fabric following layout given in instructions, placing pieces to a fold where necessary. The pattern should have a key to symbols; some patterns have perforations, meaning 'place to a fold' etc, while some have printed symbols. Check with instruction sheet as they can vary.

9 If you are not following a printed layout, cut main pieces first, facings, pockets, etc, last, when you are sure you have enough material.

10 Before cutting out, check downward cutting lines (straight grain) by measuring across from selvedge to pattern grain marks (fig 65). They should be parallel all the way along.

11 Check any pattern direction or nap and pile direction.

12 Pin pieces down so pins lie in same direction and do not obstruct

Figure 64

Figure 65

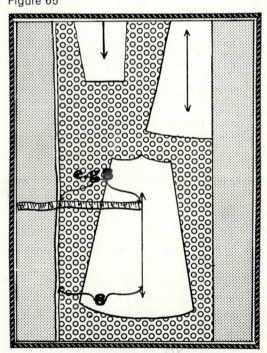

cutting lines; they should be placed about 5–7 cm apart to hold pattern without puckering fabric.

Cutting out

1 Make sure cutting scissors are sharp.
2 Keep one hand flat on table, holding material down. Cut along seam or turning allowance line of pattern (usually the solid lines), *not the fitting or stitching line* (usually the broken line). If no turning allowance is given, remember to allow for this when cutting (except where placed to a fold).
3 Put fingers in large hole, and thumb in small hole, of scissors.
4 Keep blade level with table as you cut, and cut *away* from you, keeping the material as flat as possible.
5 Don't lift material too much as this can cause mistakes.
6 When all main pieces are cut, lay them to one side so you know which have been done.
7 If any piece is to be cut double, mark darts etc, before removing pattern pieces, then transfer pattern pieces to other piece of fabric (reversing it if this is necessary).
8 Cut all corners cleanly without extending.
9 Cut notches *outwards*. Inward clipping weakens turning allowances.
10 It is advisable on easily frayed fabrics to cut extra turning allowances or edge stitch as soon as possible (see chapter 18 for seam neatening methods).
11 Leave any facings etc uncut until needed, if material frays badly.
12 Keep scraps to use as test pieces later.

Marking

Marking darts etc should be done before pattern pieces are removed from fabric pieces where possible. There are various methods of marking:

Tailor's tacks: Used on all fabrics where other marks might show permanently. Useful for marking two sections at same time. They are a very efficient method of marking. (See fig 88, chapter 7, Hand Stitches.)

Continuous tailor's tacks: Useful for marking centre backs and fronts, button placing (lengthways marks) and so on. Make tacks through all thicknesses, including paper pattern. Tear away paper pattern gently before cutting tacks. (See chapter 7 for how to make them.)

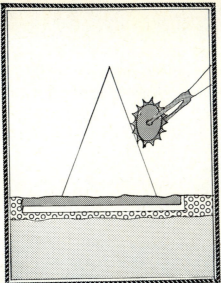

Figure 66

Using tracing wheel and paper
1 Place paper coloured side down on to wrong side of fabric.
2 Place paper pattern over tracing paper and mark off darts etc with tracing wheel or pointed end of knitting needle. Press fairly hard to make impression on to fabric.
3 Trace marks should only be made on to wrong side of fabric except for tucks and gathers.
4 For double pieces of pattern, place two sheets of tracing paper on to fabric (between the two layers) so that waxy side of one goes to wrong side of bottom layer of fabric, and waxy side of next piece of paper goes to wrong side of top layer of fabric (fig 66).

Tailor's chalk: Used for marking darts, buttonholes, etc, but should only be used on wrong side of fabric where it will not show if it does not wash out. Lift pattern piece first, pushing pins through pattern to fabric so you know where to mark.

Soft pencil marks: A 2B pencil can be used for marking lighter coloured fabrics (use on wrong side only).
1 Poke pencil point through darts, points, etc, to mark or:
2 Cut dart on paper pattern along fitting lines, pinning down at point to hold flat on fabric, then pencil round dart shape, using cut edge as a guide (remember not to cut this shape out when next using paper pattern on fabric!).

Words and terms used in this chapter (see Glossary for meanings)
Sewing terms

bias	one-way design	true cross
facings	pile	warp
layout	selvedge	weft
nap	straight grain	zig-zag
notches	tailor's tacks	

General terms

alternative	efficient	parallel
bale	extend	perforations

Things to do
1 List what you could do to prepare a loosely woven wool fabric before cutting it out.
2 List four methods of marking darts.
3 If you did not have a pattern layout for a one-way fabric, list what things you would have to take into account when devising your own layout for it.

◎ ◎ ◎

6. Helpful Hints

When you begin a needlework course there are a few tips, short-cuts, and general snippets of knowledge which it is helpful to know. This is partly to save you time and temper, and partly to give your work a professional finish. The following information should help you to avoid mistakes, and will greatly improve the look of your work.

Pressing
Always press each piece of stitching as you finish it and *before* stitching over it – eg, press shoulder darts before you stitch shoulder seams (see chapter 24, Pressing).

Pins v. tacks
Although most needlework books will tell you to pin a garment together first, then tack, it isn't always necessary to tack except

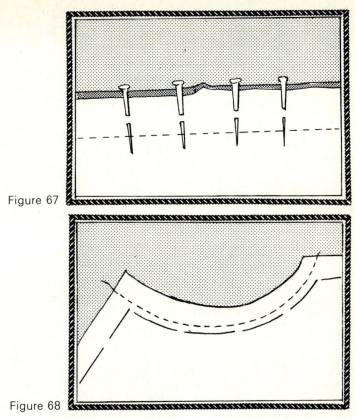

Figure 67

Figure 68

when fitting garments, where it is essential (see chapter 10, Fitting). If you decide to machine over pins, put them into the seam at right angles to the edge. This way you won't jam the machine and the pins can easily be removed later (fig 67).

Stay stitching
This means straight stitch machining round all curved or angled edges within the seam allowances, before joining any pieces together. It prevents pieces pulling out of shape, eg, necklines (fig 68).

Scrap testing
Do test out stitch and tension on a piece of scrap fabric before machining the garment. This will give an 'at a glance' guide telling you if all is well. The piece can be thrown away afterwards. To achieve a balanced stitch (fig 69a) set top machine tension to neutral

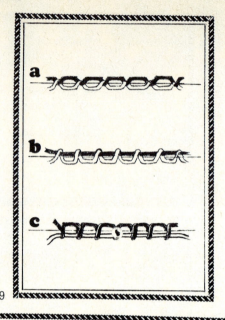

Figure 69

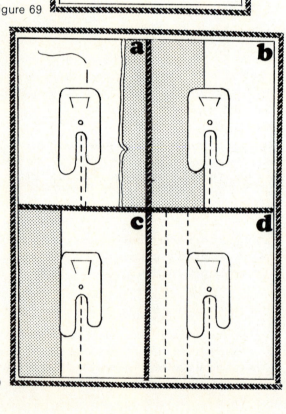

Figure 70

(see page 64) and check that machine is properly threaded before altering tensions.

1 Top thread too tight? Loosen off bobbin tension or change stitch length (fig 69b).

2 Bottom threads too tight (fig 69c)? Loosen off bobbin tension or alter stitch length.

3 Puckering of stitches on fabric? Loosen off top tension or adjust stitch length.

4 Do you suffer from wiggly stitching? Then use the edge of the ordinary presser foot as a guide.
a Inner side of small toe for machining over tacking. Keep tacking level with small toe (fig 70a).
b Inner side of large toe for machining close to folded edge. Keep fold level with large toe inner edge (fig 70b).
c Outer side of large toe for machining 0·5 cm from folded edge (useful for top stitching) (fig 70c). (Size may vary according to size of presser foot.)
d Outer side of large toe for close parallel lines (fig 70d).

5 Missing stitches? Check following:
a Needle is not blunt, bent, too loose or set too low.
b Same size thread is used on upper and lower thread.
c There is no dirt or fluff caught on needle or bobbin.
d Tension of presser foot may be too loose.
   Use a ball point needle if available, to avoid slipped stitches and tension difficulties when sewing synthetics.

Clipping curves
This is to allow the seam or join to lie flat. For outward curves, clip a v-shaped section almost to the stitching line after joining two pieces, where necessary to make it lie flat (fig 71).

Trimming angles and layering seams
Trimming outer angles means cutting them off diagonally so that when the piece is turned right side out, it lies flat. Clipping angles means snipping a line diagonally into the corner almost to the stitching line, so that when turned through it will lie flat (fig 72a).
   Layering seams, facings or edges means cutting each seam layer slightly smaller than the last so they lie flat when turned in (fig 72b).

Order of making up garments
Although the order of making up can vary slightly, the following

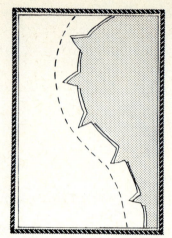

Figure 71

general rules should apply; first tack all garments together and try on for a good fit (see chapter 10, Fitting).

Dresses, blouses, jackets and coats
Remember always to press your garment as you sew.
1 Make all darts and tucks.
2 Make and attach pockets.
3 Join waist seams if applicable (if this is so, stage **6** should precede this stage).
4 Join shoulder seams and side seams, or centre back and front seams (where applicable).
5 Put in zips or fastenings (buttonloops etc).

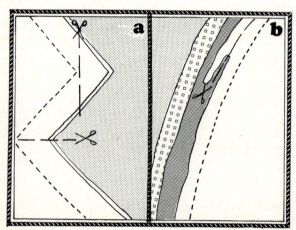

Figure 72

6 Make pleats or gathers.

7 Attach interfacings to facings and join facings to neck and front edges.

8 If collars are part of the style, make these up and attach to main garment before attaching facing.

9 Make up sleeves, then cuffs. Attach cuffs to sleeves.

10 Attach sleeves to garment.

11 Finish hems and edges.

12 Make belts etc.

Skirts

1 Make darts and tucks.

2 Make up side seams or panel seams (put zip in one seam join before attaching other pieces).

3 Make pleats or gathers.

4 Make waistbands or waist finishes and attach to main garment.

5 Finish hem (this should be finished *before pleating* if possible, if pleats are a part of the design).

Trousers

1 Make darts and tucks.

2 Join front crotch seam as far as bottom of opening (if front zip is used, put in zip).

3 Join back crotch seams (if back zip is used, put in zip).

4 Join inside leg seams all in one (on both legs).

5 Join side seams (if side zip is used, put in zip).

6 Make and attach waistband or waist finish.

7 Finish hems.

Words and terms used in this chapter (see Glossary for meanings)

Sewing terms

crotch seams	interfacings	seam allowance
darts	pleats	tucks
facings		

General terms

applicable

right angles

Things to do

List places where clipping curves and angles and layering seams might be necessary.

PART THREE
Sewing Made Simple

7. Hand Stitches

Most sewing nowadays is done by machine, but knowing a few basic hand stitches is important to enable you to make your garment properly. The following stitches are listed alphabetically so that easy stitches are not necessarily first.

ARROWHEADS (ARROWHEAD TACKS)
These are used at top of pleats etc for strength and decoration (fig 73). Use embroidery cotton in needle, of same or contrasting colour to main fabric, eg, Clark's Anchor coton à broder. Mark triangle with tailor's chalk or soft pencil on RS of work.
1 Take thread from **a** to **b** making small stitch from right to left at **b**.
2 Take thread down and insert at **c**, bringing out again at **a**, next to first stitch.

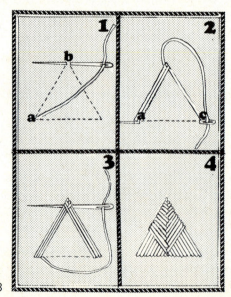

Figure 73

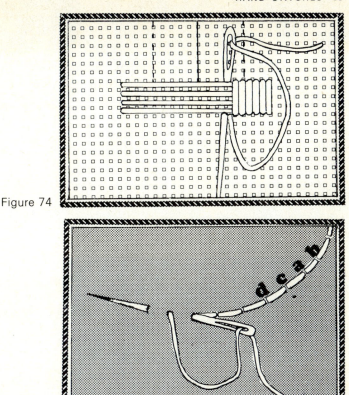

Figure 74

Figure 75

3, 4 Repeat these movements until triangle is filled. Finish with a few backstitches on ws of work.

BAR TACKS (BARS)
Strictly speaking, these are not stitches at all but a method of reinforcing pleats and openings etc which are both strong and decorative. Work from right to left (fig 74).

Method
Take three or four long stitches across end of opening working backstitch to start. Satin stitch (see page 88) across stitches evenly or use a close loop stitch as for French tacks (fig 79).

BACKSTITCH
This is a strong stitch which can be used in place of straight stitch machining. Worked correctly it looks much like a row of machining

on the RS of the work. Each stitch should be same size. Work from right to left (fig 75).

Method

1 Bring needle through on to stitching line at **a**.
2 Insert needle back, a stitch length behind.
3 Bring through to a stitch length in front.

The sequence works: **a** to **b**, **b** to **c**, **c** to **a**, **a** to **d**, and so on. Repeat to end.

BASTING

This is also known as tacking (page 90) but where the word 'baste' is used here, it refers to slanted basting (for slip basting, see page 89). This is a stitch used to hold down interfacings, linings, belt stiffenings, etc, to the main fabric. Work from top to bottom where possible (fig 76).

Method

1 Starting with a knot, insert at **a**. Bring needle out at **b**.
2 Insert needle at **c** and out at **d**. Repeat as far as desired. Long stitches should be used.

BLANKET OR LOOP STITCH

Used to neaten raw edges or to strengthen bar tacks etc, and on belt loops. Can also be used as a decorative finish. Work from left to right or right to left according to preference (fig 77).

Method

1 Work one or two backstitches to start.
2 Hold down loop with thumb and forefinger of left hand. Insert needle at **a**, bring under fabric and over loop.
3 Leave a space. Repeat to end. Finish with backstitches.

BUTTONHOLE STITCH

Used to neaten raw edges and for strengthening purposes. Work from left to right (fig 78).

Method

1 Start with a few backstitches.
2 Loop thread behind needle eye.
3 Insert needle behind work and out at point **a**, taking bottom of loop under needle point. Pull needle through and ease thread up until knot forms at raw edges of work.

CATCH STITCH

A few stitches (use slip stitches, see page 89) are taken on sections of garment to hold them down.

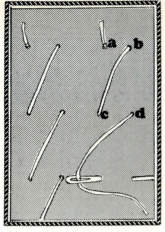

Figure 76

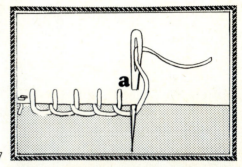

Figure 77

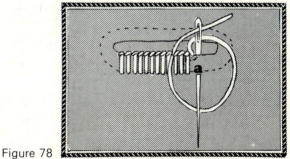

Figure 78

FRENCH TACKS
Used to hold one layer of fabric to another, whilst still allowing
some movement. They are often found between lining and garment
hems or under pleat edges (fig 79).

Method
Work a few stitches to start on one side of fabric section (slightly
up from edge for hems).
1 Take thread to corresponding place on other fabric section,

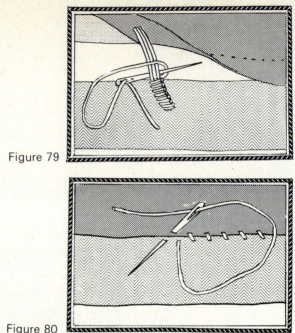

Figure 79

Figure 80

leaving about 2·5 cm between. Work three or four 'tacks' like this to form a bar.

2 Starting at one end, work loop or buttonhole stitch to other end, fasten off securely.

HEMMING STITCHES (for garment hems)
Used to hold down folded edge of fabric or garment, or to hold one piece of fabric to another if they overlap. Work from right to left (fig 80).

Method
Make very small slanted stitches picking up only a few threads of fabric and fold of hem. The smallest and most even stitches should be used as they should not show on RS of work.

HERRINGBONE STITCH
A good way of holding down hems and neatening raw edges at same time. Best used on woollen or non-frayable type fabrics worked on two thicknesses only. Work from left to right (fig 81).

Method
1 Work a few stitches to start, take thread across hem diagonally

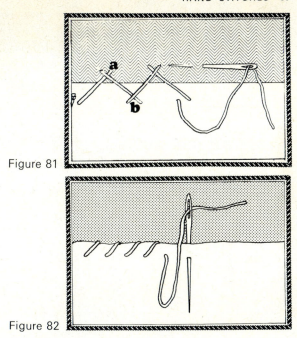

Figure 81

Figure 82

to right and *upwards,* make a small stitch at point **a.**
2 Take thread across diagonally to right *downwards* and take a
small stitch at **b.** Repeat to end. Finish with a few backstitches.

Herringbone tacking: As for above but larger stitches are taken and
stitches made across two edges of fabric to hold them together.

OVERCASTING
Used to neaten raw edges (fig 82).

Method
1 Work from left to right.
2 Start by bringing needle out of work a short distance from raw
edge. Slant needle and thread and insert needle back into work
from underneath.
3 Pull through and repeat to end. Stitches should look slanted on
both sides of work.

RUNNING STITCH
Can be used instead of backstitch, eg, for tucks, but it is not as
strong and should not be used where there might be a lot of strain.

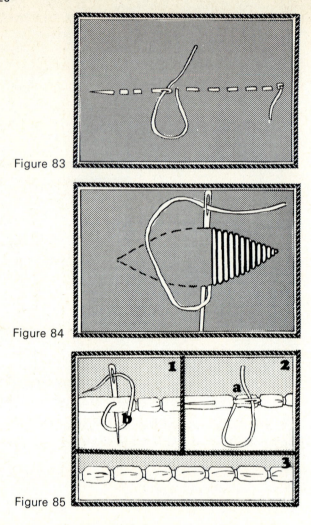

Figure 83

Figure 84

Figure 85

It is also used for gathering and easing and for marking the position of buttonholes etc. Work from right to left (fig 83).

Method
Pick up about 6 small even stitches on the needle before pulling thread through. Repeat to end.

SATIN STITCH
A decorative stitch used in embroidery and for other purposes, eg, bar tacks and appliqué (fig 84).

Method
Work straight stitches across shape required keeping stitches as close and even as possible. Do not pull up too tightly.

SHELL HEMMING
Used as a decorative hem edging on fine or sheer fabrics. Very good for transparent synthetics or cotton voiles. Work from right to left (fig 85).

Method
1 Make a very narrow double fold on to RS of work.
2 Begin with a few backstitches to hold.
3 Bring needle through centre of hem on RS. Pass needle back over hem and bring out at point **b**.
4 Take needle through loop before pulling tight. Insert needle again at **a** and slide alongside fold, bringing out some distance away to begin next stitch.

Always keep stitches an even distance from each other.

SLIP STITCH
Also known as slip hemming or slip basting. Used to hold down edges invisibly. It is a quick method for hemming and can also be useful for tacking together a seam from the RS when this is necessary

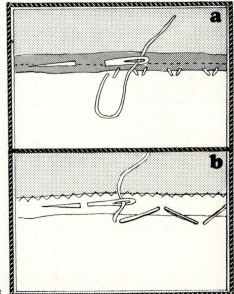

Figure 86

for matching a pattern. Work from right to left (figs 86a and b).

Method **a**: for double thickness hems
1 Fold back hem so that first turning stands up slightly, pick up a few threads on lower half of the fabric.
2 Insert needle into fold of upper half, taking a good long stitch. Pull through and pick up a few threads on lower half almost beneath this point. Repeat to end.

Method **b**: for single thickness hems
1 Fold back hem so that edge stands up. Work from right to left and pick up a few threads on lower half of fabric.
2 Insert needle into upper half, taking a small stitch. Pull needle through and take thread across to left.
3 Pick up a few threads of lower half. Repeat to end.

Tacking

Used for all stages of making up a garment where temporary stitches are needed. The quickest and easiest of all hand stitches to do. Worked from right to left, large stitches are taken along fitting lines or wherever tacking is needed. Work is started with a knot and finished with a backstitch. For extra strength, such as when tacking for a fitting, work a backstitch every 2–3 cm (fig 87).

TAILOR'S TACKS

Used for marking darts, balance points, design details, fitting lines, etc. Work from right to left.

Method **a**: Single tacks
1 Using a double thread in needle, long enough to make at least one tack and working through both (or all) thicknesses of fabric, insert needle at **a** leaving a tail and bringing out at **b**.
2 Insert again at **a** leaving a good sized loop. Bring out at **b** and

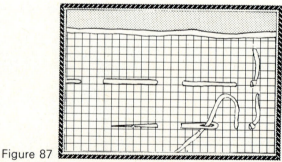

Figure 87

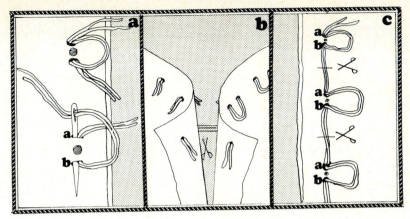

Figure 88

cut off thread about 5 cm away (fig 88a).

Cutting: Carefully and slowly pull sections apart until you feel a tug. Cut through stitches between two sections of fabric. Both pieces should now have tufts of thread showing (fig 88b).

Method **b**: For continuous tailor's tacks
Same as for plain tailor's tacks, but make a row of tacks along line to be marked, *without cutting until end*. You must leave good sized loops for this (fig 88c).

For more information on tailor's tacks and marking processes see chapter 5.

WHIP STITCHING
Similar to overcasting but is used to join together edges of non-fraying fabric or garment sections which have already had their edges neatened, eg, patchwork. Work from right to left (fig 89).

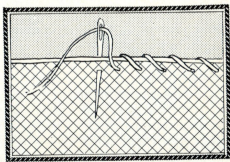

Figure 89

Method
Begin a short distance from edge. Take thread across diagonally to right. Insert needle behind both layers of fabric and bring out at **b**. Repeat to end. Stitches show slanted on one side and at right angles to edge on other side.

Golden rules for hand stitches

1 Use right thread for the stitch and the work it must do, eg, either Coats' Drima, an all-purpose thread, or Coats' Satinised 40 and 50 (mercerized cotton) for hand and machine sewing on natural fabrics; Coats' Drima (polyester) for synthetic fabrics; Anchor embroidery threads.
2 Do not pull stitches too tight (except shell hemming) as this causes puckering.
3 Use small neat, even stitching where applicable, especially if showing from RS.
4 Stitches for holding down hems, facings, etc, should be so small as to be practically invisible on RS of work. The secret is to take only a few threads on the RS section and a much longer stitch on the hem edge. This will therefore be both quick and neat.
5 Begin and end all stitches (except temporary ones) with a back-stitch or oversewing for strength on hems especially.

Words and terms used in this chapter (see Glossary for meanings)

Sewing terms

appliqué	gathering	synthetics
easing	interfacing	tailor's chalk
fitting line	linings	tucks
fray(able)	patchwork	voile

General terms

continuous	forefinger	sheer
contrasting	reinforcing	temporar(y)(ily)
corresponding	sequence	triangle
diagonally		

Things to do

1 List three places where you might use overcasting stitch.
2 List three or more places where you might use tailor's tacks and for what reason.
3 List which hand stitches could be used for embroidery as well as for other purposes.

8. Crossway

Definition: Any fabric cut to an exact 45° angle from the selvedge or straight grain.

Fabric cut on the true cross will stretch more and be more 'elastic' than fabric cut on the straight grain. For this reason it is ideal for many purposes in dressmaking: facings, bindings, piping, soft collars, rouleaux, etc. These are often cut on the cross so that they can stretch round curved or shaped areas and lie well.

Crossway can be used for a decorative effect on pockets, cuffs and collars. Even plain skirts and bodices can look original if the fabric is patterned and cut on the cross (fig 90).

The term 'bias' can be confusing as it really has two meanings. Commercial bias binding is a binding cut on the true 45° cross but the word *bias* in sewing really means fabric *cut at any degree off the straight grain*. Paper patterns which say 'bias cut' usually mean that the dress or skirt is cut on the true cross to allow a very clinging fit or the maximum stretch to the fabric.

To make crossway binding, piping or narrow facings, you must

Figure 90

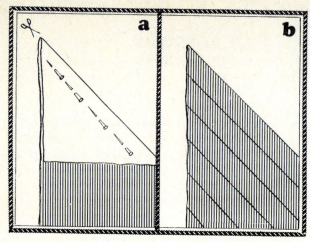

Figure 91

know how to cut and join crossway strips. After a few attempts you will get the hang of it.

Crossway strips are often cut from pieces of spare fabric, and it is not always possible to know where the straight grain is. To find out, pull a thread from the fabric in each direction and cut along these marks. This should give a perfect right-angle in one corner which can be used as a guide.

Method for cutting crossway
1 Fold one edge straight across to the other, with edges parallel.
2 Pin along close to fold and press fold with fingers so that a crease

Figure 91

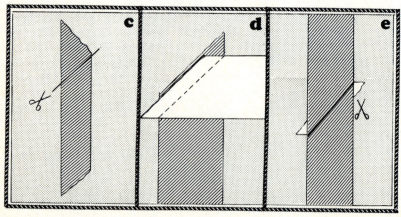

forms. Using sharp scissors, cut into crease along its length and unpin (fig 91a). You will now have two pieces of fabric each with a guideline to the true cross.

3 Pin or chalk mark a line parallel to the diagonal all along, keeping depth even (a 2·5 cm crossway is a useful size, but narrower or wider can be measured off). The strips must be of equal depth for good joins (fig 91b).

4 Cut near pins or along chalk mark. A ruler and soft pencil will also make a good marker for crossway. Use ruler as a width guide and pencil to mark fabric along its length. Move ruler so far edge rests on pencil line and draw another line. Repeat until enough strips are marked off.

Method for joining crossway

1 Cut each end of each strip along straight grain (follow line of weave), noting that each strip should look like a parallelogram (fig 91c).

2 Place one strip right side up, and vertical, on a flat surface. Place joining strip right side down on top of it and at right angles to it. The raw edges of diagonals will meet and each piece will have a triangular overlap at one end.

3 Tack and machine strips together, making sure that machine line goes exactly to corners for a good finish (fig 91d).

4 Open out strip, press seam open and trim off two surplus pieces (fig 91e).

Cutting and joining a continuous crossway strip

A useful quick method to know if you need to make a lot of crossway strips (eg, when facing or binding hems etc). It will give a perfect join.

1 Pull threads to find the straight grain of fabric. It may be necessary to pull threads along four sides if there is no selvedge guide.

2 Fold warp to weft so that two raw edges are together. Pin and crease fold. Remove pins and cut through crease line. This will give first guide.

3 Measure off with a pencil or chalk, a series of strips all the way down on wrong side, *but do not cut*. Repeat to end of piece of fabric and cut away triangle of excess fabric at each end (fig 92a).

4 Fold fabric into a tube (RS together), matching raw edges but moving fabric so that a single depth of crossway is left free at each end (see points **A** and **B**, fig 92b). Tack and machine.

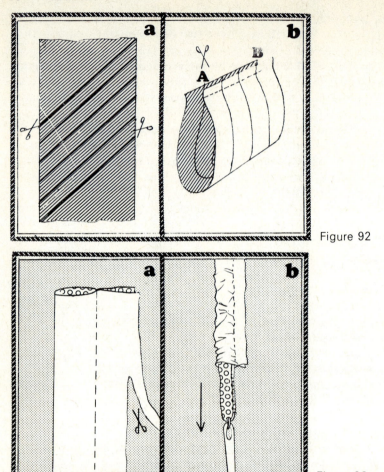

Figure 92

Figure 93

5 Starting at point **A**, cut along fabric, following chalk marks. The crossway forms a spiral so you will continue cutting until you reach the end, point **B** (fig 92b).

Rouleaux

A 'rouleau' just means a *tube of fabric*. Padded with cord, it is known as corded rouleau; left unpadded, it is known as soft rouleau. It has numerous uses; lacing, ties, buttonloops, belts, decorative finishes and so on. It is easy to make once you know all the tricks involved and it looks very attractive. (The plural of rouleau is rouleaux.)

Method for soft rouleaux (uncorded)
1 Cut and join crossway strip the length and twice the width of required rouleau (plus turnings).
2 Placing right sides and raw edges together, tack and machine parallel to edge along its length. Trim surplus turnings (fig 93a).
3 Measure off length of piping cord same length as finished rouleau and narrow enough to go through it. Stitch bodkin or hairgrip to one end of cord. Stitch other end of cord to one end of rouleau, being careful not to close tube.
4 Push bodkin through tube to other end and ease rouleau back over cord. This should enable rouleau to be turned through successfully (fig 93b).
5 Cut off cord and oversew raw edges of tube.

Method for corded rouleaux
This is exactly the same procedure as for soft rouleaux, except that twice the length of cord is needed for each tube, and it should be large enough in diameter to pad it comfortably.
   Repeat as for soft rouleaux to stage **4**, then cut off excess cord (the rest should be filling the rouleau). Oversew firmly at each end.

Using crossway on curved edges
For bindings or facings crossway often has to be eased or stretched to fit a curve.

Convex curves: These are outer curves, eg, hems. The outer edge

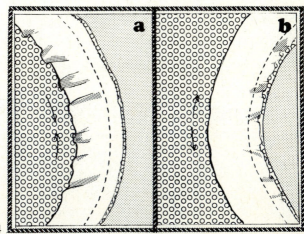

Figure 94

should be slightly stretched and inner edge eased so that crossway lies flat (fig 94a).

Concave curves: These are inward curves found, for example, at neck edge. Neck or inner edge should be eased so outer edge lies flat (fig 94b).

Final joins on continuous or circular edges
Found at hems, armholes or necks without back or front openings. The join should be made before crossway strip is machined in place.
1 Tack strip to last few cm each side of join.
2 Crease back a turning on to one end of strip on straight grain. Crease back a turning on other strip so two ends meet in perfect match and lie flat on garment.
3 Trim off surplus fabric from one turning (fig 95).
4 Tack and machine two ends together using crease mark as guide. Remove tacks and press open.
5 Complete tacking of strip to garment.

For rouleaux buttonloops, see chapter 14.
For crossway bindings and pipings, see chapters 20 and 21.
For crossway facings, see chapter 19.

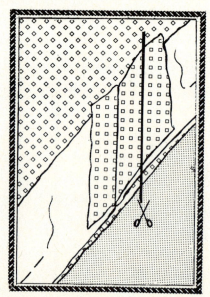

Figure 95

For more information on crossway, see chapter 12, pages 136–137.

Golden rules for crossway

1 Cut crossway strips needed from spare pieces of main fabric if possible, if not, cut from a similar weight fabric (but heavy wools etc need finer material for crossway pipings).
2 Check you are cutting on the true cross, that is at a 45° angle from the warp or weft (straight grain).
3 Cut strips wide enough for the job they must do.
4 Cut strips evenly along the length and use a measure to mark off identical width strips for joining.
5 If fabric has a right and wrong side, take account of this when joining and applying crossway.

Words and terms used in this chapter (see Glossary for meanings)

Sewing terms

bodkin	straight grain	weave
rouleau(x)	warp	weft
selvedge		

General terms

commercial	numerous	spiral
diagonal	parallel	surplus
diameter	parallelogram	triangular

Things to do

1 Cut and join a sample crossway strip.
2 List at least four different uses for crossway. Make up one of these in a sample.
3 Design and draw a dress or other garment using crossway cut fabric as a feature.

◎   ◎   ◎

9. Interfacings and Linings

These two processes have been bracketed together in the same chapter, not because they *are* the same, but because each performs a similar function and neither is seen from the right side of the garment.

You will find that however simple a garment you are making, it will probably need an interfacing or interlining somewhere, and for many garments you will need to line part of them for a professional and neat finish.

Interfacings

Definition: Any material which is used between the top layer of the garment fabric and an underneath layer such as a facing or hem.

Interfacings are used in various places and for various reasons.
1 They give 'body' and crispness to the part of the garment they are used in, eg, a hem.
2 They stop certain parts from stretching out of shape, eg, a faced neck edge.
3 They make certain parts more hard-wearing, eg, cuffs.
4 They generally improve the whole look of a garment and actually make the processes and techniques of dressmaking easier by preventing certain parts of the garment from slipping around, eg, a collar anchored (whilst working) by iron-on interfacing.

There are two types of interfacing: the woven kind, which can be plain type or iron-on (these include canvas, horsehair, voile, organdie, etc) and the non-woven types such as the bonded fabrics (eg, Vilene) which can also be obtained as plain or iron-on.

Woven interfacing

If you use a woven interfacing, you must be sure the grain is straight before cutting (for straightening, see chapter 5, under Preparing the fabric) and that it is pre-shrunk, if it is to be used in a garment which is to be washed. If the interfacing is not pre-shrunk, then use the method given in chapter 5 for shrinking fabrics.

When you cut woven interfacings always cut pattern pieces on the straight grain (see chapter 5) and place interfacing on garment section, matching straight grain to straight grain. This is vitally important as a badly placed interfacing can pull a garment completely out of shape. The only exception to this is if the pattern piece is cut on the cross in which case the interfacing must also be cut on the cross.

Place the interfacing piece to garment piece on wrong side and slip baste (see chapter 7) into position. (Remember to remove slip basting stitches at end.) Catch stitch using small, invisible stitches

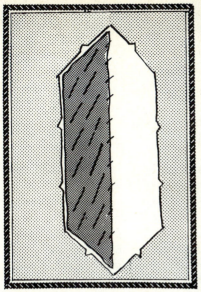

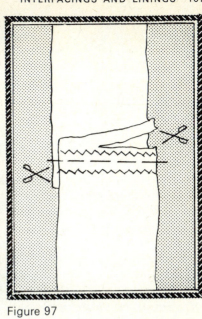

Figure 96   Figure 97

along any folds (fig 96). (This isn't necessary if fold is to be machined or stitched afterwards.) Make up garment as usual when interfacing has been attached.

Non-woven interfacing
Because this has no grain line, it can be cut in any direction and is therefore very economical. Place in position and baste down as for woven types.

Iron-on interfacings
If these are woven, be careful to cut on the straight grain of the pattern piece. If they are not, cut from any part but remember that only one side has the glue on it. If you have to interface two pieces of a neckline, pattern should be reversed for one piece. Be careful when ironing on ws of fabric not to get fabric rucked up underneath.

Joining interfacing
Because it doesn't show on the garment at all, it doesn't matter if you have a join or two on the interfacing and this is sometimes necessary for economy's sake. For both the woven and non-woven types lay one section over the other on fitting line, and straight

stitch or zig-zag together a short way from this line on each side. Trim away surplus fabric from each piece (fig 97). For iron-on types just overlap one section on to the other matching fitting lines and iron gently until bonded.

Linings

Definition: Any extra material which is used on the inside of the garment, which makes it hang better, stops it creasing or prevents it being 'see-throughable', and allows for easy movement in wear.

For very fine or sheer materials a lining is often essential, not merely for modesty's sake, but to give some 'body' to the garment and to make it harder wearing. There are many kinds of lining fabric; a lining doesn't necessarily have to be made from a slippery fabric at all. A good lining for a sheer fabric could be a cotton voile or organdie. Remember that if the garment is washable the lining should be fully washable too. A lining fabric should be of the same weight or lighter than the main fabric, but never heavier.

There are two main methods of lining a garment: the first one is called *mounting* (or interlining) and this is probably the easiest way of all to line something or to give it body. It means cutting out the lining pieces and making them up at the same time and with the main garment pieces – as if you were working with one piece of fabric. Of course, although this gives the garment extra weight and body,

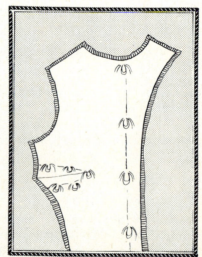

Figure 98

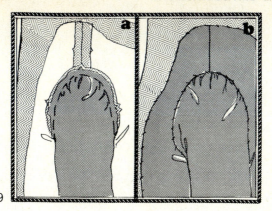

Figure 99

it does nothing to hide the raw edges inside, so these must be neatened in some way.

If you wish to mount a garment with lining (it is almost the same as interfacing it) use the following method:

Method
1 Cut main piece first.
2 Move pattern pieces to mounting fabric and cut these out too.
3 Place ws of mounting to ws of garment fabric.
4 Replace pattern pieces and mark off balance points, darts, etc, with tailor's tacks, through both thicknesses of fabric (fig 98).
5 To prevent two pieces slipping apart, catch stitch them every so often or slip baste (see chapter 7). If fabrics are not too slippery, one can be laid on top of the other (be careful on double sections) ws together, and pattern pieces cut through all thicknesses.

When using ordinary lining various methods may be used, eg, garment is first made up, then linings made separately. The two are joined together afterwards. If this is the case sometimes only half a lining is used, eg, a skirt which is lined only at the back or halfway down, to thigh level.

Alternatively:
Couture method: For coats, dresses or jackets with sleeves.
1 Make up sleeves.
2 Make up sleeve linings.
3 Press under a hem on sleeve lining (to ws) and pin and tack sleeve linings to main garment sleeves (ws together) at hems. Slip stitch in

place, remove tacks. Attach sleeve linings to main sleeves at arm-hole edge also, but be sure they are not pulling. Gather up sleeve heads as normal, through both thicknesses.

4 Make up main garment in full attaching sleeves (complete with lining) to body (fig 99a).

5 Attach lining to main part (ws together) making up hem and attaching in places with bar tacks (see chapter 7) (fig 100).

6 Turn under raw edges of lining at armholes on to the sleeve and tack in place.

7 Try garment on to check nothing is pulling.

8 Slip stitch armholes to sleeves; remove all tacks (fig 99b).

LINING A SKIRT

Method 1: Full lining.

1 Make up skirt main parts and lining main parts (omitting waist-band or waistline facing). The hem should be made on the lining beforehand where possible as it is easier to handle.

2 Place ws of lining to ws of skirt, pin and tack at waist edge, making sure that it fits. For zips and openings leave the right length un-stitched in lining seam. Turn under raw edges and stitch these to edge of opening of garment making sure nothing is catching (fig 101a).

3 Remove pins and machine on fitting line of waist through all

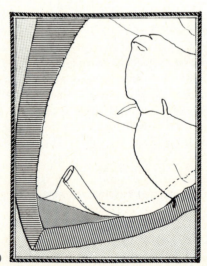

Figure 100

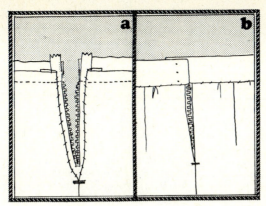

Figure 101

thicknesses. Attach waistband or waist finish as usual (fig 101b).
Note: If it was not possible to make up hem of the lining before attaching it to main garment, tack it up and machine it at the last stage (pull lining away from the main garment to avoid catching the material in the machining).

Method 2: Half lining.
This can be made to line back of skirt only, or both front and back, (to avoid creases across stomach). The only variation from a full

Figure 102

Figure 103

lining is that it doesn't go the whole length of the skirt but finishes at hip level, or just below, to stop the skirt 'seating' (fig 102).

PLEATS AND OPENINGS IN SKIRTS

If the skirt or dress has a back pleat or slit opening, it is best either to make a centre back seam in the lining and only complete this to the top of garment pleat etc, leaving rest open (fig 103) or make the lining only as far as the top of the pleat or opening, so avoiding the problem altogether. In this case, if the opening in the skirt is a slit opening, it is best to make a Dior flap (see chapter 11).

LINING BODICES

You can either line these by the same construction as given for coats and jackets (if the dress has sleeves) or as given for the all-in-one bodice and neck facing method, chapter 19, if it is sleeveless, and attach lining at waist after completing armhole and neck edges.

Words and terms used in this chapter (see Glossary for meanings)

Sewing terms

balance marks	interfacing	mounting
facing	interlining	seam allowance
fitting line	lining(s)	tailor's tacks

General terms

construction	omitting	pre-shrunk

Things to do
1 Explain why interfacing is necessary and where.
2 Collect scraps of interfacings and linings in various weights and fabrics. List a few notes about them at the side of each. Give possible uses and reasons for choice.
3 Explain why a lining is necessary and say where you would use it.

◎   ◎   ◎

10. Fitting

If you have used the right patterns for size and figure type, you should not need to make many alterations. Occasionally, however, some changes are necessary after the garment is cut out. This entails a process called fitting.

Fitting should be done before joining any of the seams permanently so that any alterations are easy to do. Either tack the main pieces together for fitting (using a backstitch at each end of the seam for strength), or set the machine to the *largest* stitch and machine the seams together using *tacking* thread. It should be fairly easy to undo any machine tacking. A second fitting should be made *after* the main seams are machined together permanently and *before* placing any collar or facings on etc, just to check that everything is where it should be.

Figure 104

Some points before you start

1 When fitting get a friend to help (fig 104) as she can probably see better than you the whole effect, or use a full length three-sided mirror to see the side and back views of garment and how it is hanging.

2 Wear the underclothes you intend to wear with the garment. This makes a great deal of difference to the hang of it. When the garment is finished, don't wear it with the wrong underwear, eg, a top with cut-away shoulders showing bra straps.

3 If dress has a belt incorporated in it, wear this when trying on dress for final fitting. This can entirely alter the shape and length of dress.

4 Wear shoes or boots when fitting (the ones you would normally wear with the garment) as this can affect the hang of the hem.

5 Try garment on for fitting RS outside as your left side may not be exactly the same size and shape as the right-hand side of your body.

Some points about fitting

Note: For all pattern alterations see chapter 2.

1 *Shoulder seam*: Check slope of shoulder seam. It may need to be curved in slightly or let out. Wrinkles forming across back at armhole? Shoulder seam may be too short and should be lengthened. Wrinkles forming across shoulder seam? It probably needs to be shortened. Wrinkles from shoulder to bust? Shoulder seam needs to be lengthened at armhole edge. Wrinkles from neckline to arm-hole? Shoulder seam needs shortening at armhole.

2 *The neckline*: Is it too tight or too loose? Too tight and wrinkles will form across base of neck; let out shoulder seams at neckline and

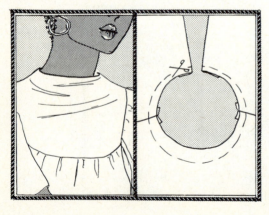

Figure 105

Figure 106

Figure 107

cut neckline down slightly at front in a gentle curve; adjust collar or facing to fit new size (fig 105). Too loose – wrinkles form lengthways and neck will hang in folds. Take in neckline at seams or shrink neckline as for shrinking hems if fabric will take it (see chapter 23, Hems). It can also be gathered slightly if the design will allow it (fig 106).

3 *Darts*: Are darts placed correctly, do the points of the darts come where they should (over the fullest part of body)? Points of bust darts coming *above* fullest part of bust means they are too high and should be lowered (fig 107a). To do this, keep wide part of dart at same point, but reset dart point (fig 107b). Points of bust darts coming below fullest part of bust means they are set too low and should be lifted (fig 108a and b). Dart point tending to poke out means it is made too straight; darts should curve when they are made to go over curving parts of body (see chapter 11, under Darts).

4 *Waistline seam*: Is it in the right place or does it pull at back or

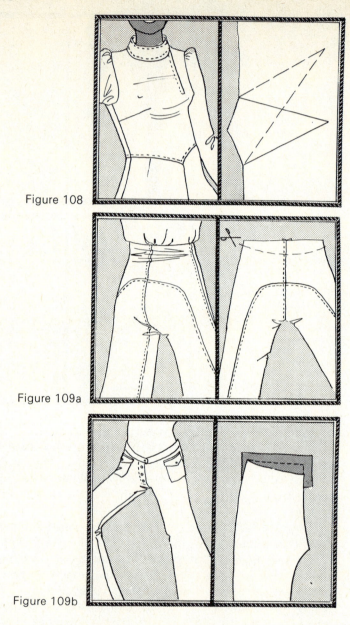

Figure 108

Figure 109a

Figure 109b

front? Wrinkles going across stomach or small part of back means waistline is not fitting correctly. Let out at side seams or cut a new curve at waistline. This means lowering the waistline at centre

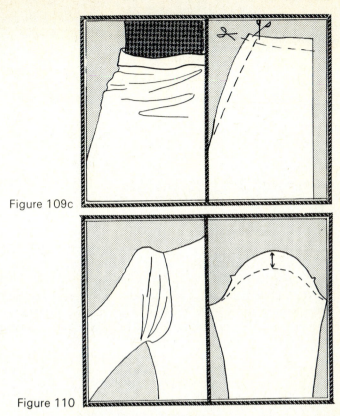

Figure 109c

Figure 110

front and back (fig 109a). Waistline pulling down at back or front means it needs lifting – add extra piece of tissue to pattern and draw in new waistline curve slightly above old, keeping sides same level but raising centre front and back seams (fig 109b). If material has already been cut, try to gain this extra amount from seam allowance of waist join. Trousers with this problem? They may need making larger at front or back. Check crotch measurements with measurements of pattern before cutting out (see chapter 2). Waistline hanging in folds across body but not pulling, means it may need excess fabric taken up at waistline. Do same as for lowering waistline, taking up excess at side seams too (fig 109c).

5 *Sleeves*: Does the sleeve head (crown of sleeve) fit properly or does it pull or go in wrinkles? Too tight it means wrinkles will form lengthways across upper arm. Cut sleeve head slightly larger in a more generous curve. If material has already been cut, try to gain extra amount from top seam allowance (fig 110). Sometimes wrinkles

form across the arm because the sleeve is too small and too short, and may need lengthening and widening; or sleeve may hang loosely because it is too large and too long, and may need shortening and making narrower. See chapter 2, under Pattern Alterations.

Words and terms used in this chapter (see Glossary for meanings)
Sewing terms

crotch measurement	pattern size	sleeve head (crown)
figure type	seam allowance	

General terms

incorporated	tapered off

Things to do
1 List places for fitting the garment *before* making up the main seams permanently.
2 List possible places garment may have to be fitted *after* making up main seams.
3 Make up a toile to a basic pattern, get a friend to help you fit it, and see how and where it differs from the main pattern. (A toile can be made of really cheap, poor quality material as it is only for fitting purposes.)

PART FOUR

Basic Methods

The following basic methods give instructions for working some of the most important processes in needlework. You may find eventually through experience, that a technique or method of your own works best for you for a particular process. However, those given in the text are a guide for the beginner.

11. Adjustment of Fullness

DARTS, PLEATS, TUCKS AND GATHERS

Unless clothes are made as straight up and down tubes, or made with many shaped seam panels, then at some stage or other excess material has to be removed or rearranged in such a way that a garment fits what it is supposed to fit. Apart from the shaped seams mentioned, there are four other main ways of tackling this problem and it is likely that one or the other of these processes will be one of the first things to be done when you start to make a garment.

The four ways are: darts, tucks, pleats (most of these lie comparatively flat or smooth) and gathers (these are bulky but can be made flatter by using smocking stitches).

Darts
Definition: A method of shaping. Part of the fabric is taken in and held together by stitching on the wrong side some distance from the fold. One or both ends of the dart are tapered to a point.

Darts give shape and definition to a garment and allow a smooth contoured effect which follows the line of the body at certain points (fig 111). They are usually used:
1 At front and back bodice at waist level.
2 At front bodice underarm going towards bust point.
3 At back, neck or shoulders.
4 At sleeve heads, elbows or wrists.
5 From waist to hips on back and front skirt or trouser sections.

Figure 111

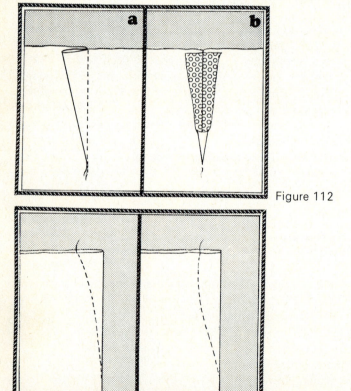

Figure 112

Figure 113

Most darts are made on the wrong side of the work but occasionally, as part of the style, they can be made on the right side. Some darts have two pointed ends, eg, at waist shaping of dresses and jackets, some are curved to fit certain parts of the body and some are found at hems and are known as dart tucks.

STRAIGHT DARTS
Used at front underarm (bust dart), skirt and bodice back, shoulder, elbow and wrist.

Method
1 Mark off position of dart on ws of garment.
2 Fold along centre of dart RS together, bringing marks of each side together. Pin and tack in a straight line from dart point to widest part.
3 Remove pins. Machine carefully starting from widest part and tapering to almost nothing for last few cm. Remove tacks and press to one side (fig 112a).

All vertical darts should be pressed towards centre back or front. All horizontal darts should be pressed downwards. Very bulky fabrics should have darts slit almost to the point and pressed open (neaten edges to avoid fraying) (fig 112b).

CURVED DARTS
There are two types of curved darts: those which curve in and those which curve out. Inward curving darts are usually used on skirt and trouser fronts, from waist to hips. Outward curving darts are usually used at the waist of dress bodice fronts, or fitted jackets seamed at the waist.

Method
Repeat the same procedure as for straight darts but curve tacking and machining very slightly along first $\frac{2}{3}$ of dart, keeping last part straight and tapering to nothing (fig 113).

DOUBLE-POINTED DARTS
Used on dresses and jackets without waist seams, and hip level overblouses and shirts. Curved double-pointed darts can be used for front sections of garments but great care should be taken to keep curves smooth.

Method: For straight double-pointed darts.
1 Mark off position of dart on garment section (ws).
2 Fold along centre of dart RS together. Pin and tack down, keeping

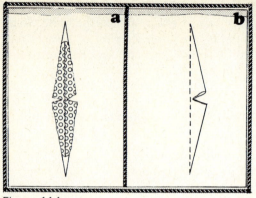

Figure 114

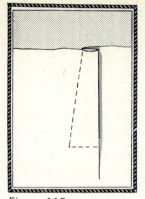

Figure 115

stitching straight from centre to points, tapering to nothing at ends.
3 Remove pins and machine dart on tacking line.
4 Remove tacks. Clip darts at centre. Press to one side (fig 114b)
or slit centre fold of each dart almost to points and press open;
neaten edges (fig 114a).

DART TUCKS
Used on blouse fronts and backs.

Method
1 Mark position of dart on ws.
2 Crease along centre fold (RS inside) bringing marks together. Pin
and tack dart.
3 Remove pins. Machine on fitting line from narrow end (hem level)
to farthest point at wide end. Then machine straight across fold.
Press (fig 115).

FINISHING
Finish off all ends of darts by either tying off, stitching in, or
machining back over stitching at each end. Trim off threads.

Pleats
Definition: A fold taken into the fabric and laid across its own width
on remainder of the fabric (fig 116).

Pleats can be one of the smartest and most successful methods of
adjusting fullness. They are used on skirts, dresses, jackets, blouses
and even trousers. There are various kinds of pleats, but the main
ones are: knife, box, inverted, sunray and accordion.

Figure 116

Pleats are formed after the seams are joined if they are to be made all round the width of the garment; or made before making up garment sections, eg, centre back pleat of a shirt joined to a yoke. Where possible hems should be completed before pleats are made and any seam joins should be hidden under a pleat.

When tacking use silk or fine thread to avoid marking, as tacking should be left in until pressing is complete. When all pleats are made up, press with iron and damp cloth.

KNIFE PLEAT

This is a fold taken to one side of the fabric and either partly stitched down or left free. Knife pleats are often made in groups or all the way round the garment, eg, a knife-pleated skirt.

Method

1 Mark position of pleats on garment or garment section. Three marks are necessary for each pleat (fig 117a):

   (A) to mark fold of pleat
   (B) to mark point where fold should come
   (C) to mark where fold should come on ws. This will be half the width between **A** and **B**.

2 Fold and lightly press all way down at point **A**. Bring point **A** to point **B** (fig 117b).

3 Tack through all thicknesses at fold. If pleats are to be stitched part way down, this is done before joining the pleated section to

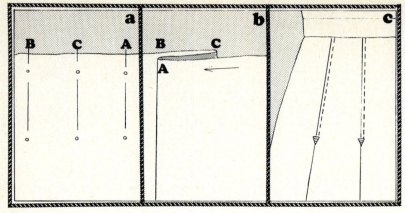

Figure 117

another section. Length to be machined is marked off on each pleat and a row of machining made close to the fold of pleat on the RS of garment. Finish end of each row of stitching with an arrowhead tack (see chapter 7) (fig 117c).

BOX PLEAT
These are two knife pleats next to, but facing away from, each other. They can be made in groups around a garment, eg, a skirt, but give a boxy, squarish shape, so are best avoided if you have a tendency

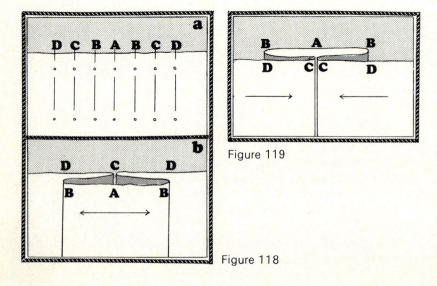

Figure 119

Figure 118

to plumpness. They are more often used singly and left unstitched, eg, centre back pleat of a shirt.

Method
1 Mark position of pleats on RS of garment (fig 118a).
   (A) centre point
   (B) outer folds point
   (C) inner folds point
   (D) point where outer fold comes on RS.
2 Crease fabric all the way down at point **B** (fig 118b).
3 Reverse crease fabric all the way down at point **C** (fig 118b).
4 Bring fold points **B** to points **D** at each side (fig 118b).
5 Tack in place. Press. Remove tacks after making up garment.

INVERTED PLEAT
An inverted pleat is identical to a box pleat but is made back to front, ie, made on the WS of the garment rather than the RS. Inverted pleats are often used at skirt or jacket backs or anywhere ease of movement is necessary.

Repeat the same procedure as for a box pleat but on *wrong side* of the garment (fig 119).

KICK PLEATS
These are really knife pleats with the fold of the material going only part of the way up the garment. They can only be made into a seam. For instance, the centre back seam of a skirt. Often a pattern will be especially cut to incorporate a kick pleat within the design.

Method
1 Join seam RS together (fig 120a).

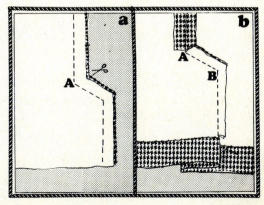

Figure 120

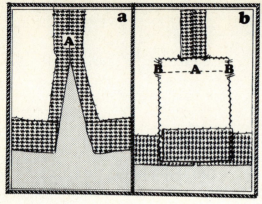

Figure 121

2 Clip seam at point **A** and press open to top (fig 120b).

3 Press seam to one side and stitch from point **A** to point **B** through all thicknesses making sure that pleat lies flat (fig 120b).

4 Turn up, and finish hem before giving pleat a final press on RS.

FALSE PLEATS (sometimes known as Dior flaps)
These are not really pleats at all, but extra flaps of material placed beneath an opening. They look like inverted pleats from the RS and are very useful for skirts etc.

Method
1 Make up skirt or garment, including hem. Leave an opening where flap is to go (fig 121a).

2 Press open centre 'pleat' seam (slip stitch turnings down).

3 Cut fabric for flap and finish three raw edges, ie, top and two sides (using binding, zig-zag or overcasting).

4 Position centre fitting line of top of flap to point **A** on garment (about 2·5 cm above top of opening). Pin and tack from **A** to **B** each side, keeping flap as flat as possible on garment (fig 121b).

5 Catch stitch flap to garment on seam at centre and at each side (fig 121b).

6 Mark hem position on flap (it should be same length as garment or fractionally shorter but never longer) and finish hem of flap (fig 121b). Remove tacks.

ACCORDION AND SUNRAY PLEATS
These both have the folds raised so that the pleats do not lie flat but stand up. Sunray pleats have tapered ends at waist level which widen out towards the hem. Both kinds of pleat have to be made by

a special method using chemicals and pressing techniques during the making up of the fabric. It is not possible for the home dressmaker to make them (unless she has stolen a few secret formulae from ICI!).

Tucks
Definition: A fold is made in the fabric on the right or wrong side and held in place by machining through both thicknesses of the fold. It is not machined down to the garment (fig 122).

Tucks differ from darts in that they do not have tapered ends and are really a means of getting rid of fullness rather than shaping to a particular contour. Some tucks do not go the whole length of the garment section but stop short, allowing the remaining fabric to fall in unpressed pleats, eg, fronts of smock-shaped dresses etc.

Tucks can be made horizontal, vertical or both. They can even be made on the cross, but vertical tucks are the easiest to make as they lie flat whilst making up. Some tucks are wide and some are so narrow they are known as pin tucks. The very narrow tucks can be corded to give them a raised look.

Some very attractive effects can be gained by using tucked sections on garments, but if you are making these (eg, at collar, cuffs or yoke), rather than try to estimate the amount of extra material needed at the cutting out stage, it is better to make up a

Figure 122

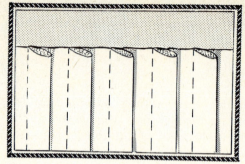

Figure 123

piece of tucked material first, then cut the garment piece(s) from this.

Pin tucks can be made automatically by using a twin needle in the machine and two reels of thread. Some very interesting permutations can be made by combining twin needle with zig-zag or other swing needle stitches. Try some on a practice piece of fabric but do remember to set the dials to *half* the usual width of the stitch being tried, to avoid breaking the needles.

As well as for decoration and removing width fullness, tucks can be used to allow shortening and lengthening on garments, whilst still looking attractive. They can also hide joins in material. You can buy special plastic cards called tuckmarkers, or you can make your own from stiff card. They have a similar use to a hem gauge, in that they measure off an even width along a length of fabric.

Method for narrow tucks
1 Crease material to width required (ws together if making on to rs of garment). Pin and tack in place.
2 Either machine tucks parallel to fold or use a small running stitch by hand (see chapter 7, Hand Stitches).
3 Measure off next tuck with a marker and repeat above procedure.
4 Repeat as many times as required. Then press tucks in one direction only (usually away from centre for vertical tucks, or downwards for horizontal tucks) (fig 123).

Method for wider tucks
Use same procedure but mark off tucks all the way along with tacks or tracing paper marks first, as any unevenness will be likely to show more on wider tucks.

Gathering
Definition: Excess material is drawn up to less width by means of

hand or machine gathering stitches, eg, running stitch or machine straight stitch (fig 124).

If you make your own clothes it is likely that gathering is a process that you will encounter at some stage of every garment you make. Gathers are the easiest way to adjust fullness, but to look professional the folds forming in the material when the gathering threads are drawn up should be evenly distributed.

Gathers can be used on skirts; (at waist level) on dress or blouse bodice sections; beneath back and front yokes, on sleeve heads and cuffs, and on frills of all kinds.

The following methods for gathering are the most usual.

HAND GATHERING

1 Mark off sections to be gathered, at each end.

2 Make a row of small running stitches from one point to another on marked line (fitting line usually) starting with some firm back-stitches and leaving thread free at other end.

3 Work another row 0·3 cm above the first.

4 Pull two threads and draw up gathered section to fit required size, eg, a 20 cm yoke section will require a 20 cm gathered section. Secure threads by looping around a pin (in a figure of eight) inserted in end (fig 125).

5 Adjust gathers to fall evenly.

Figure 124

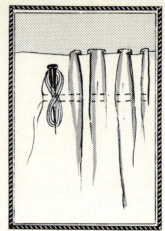

Figure 125

6 Join gathered section to its matching piece.
7 Do not remove running stitches until sections are permanently joined. Press seam lightly, all thicknesses to go in one direction. (For overlaid seams see chapter 12.)

MACHINE-MADE GATHERS
1 Mark off section to be gathered.
2 Set machine stitch length dial or lever to longest stitch.
3 Machine along fitting line between marked points to be gathered.
4 Machine 0·3 cm above this line.
5 Fasten at one end all gathering threads, then pull up free ends at other end to fit required size. Only bobbin thread (underneath one) need be pulled to make gathers.
7 Arrange gathers and secure threads.

Some machines will gather automatically and these are fine for long sections of gathers such as frills. Try out gathering stitch first on a spare piece of fabric.

Shirring
Definition: A number of rows of gathering using threads only, or thread *and* narrow tubular elastic (fig 126).

Shirring can be used as a design feature purely for decoration (threads only), giving a similar effect to smocking especially if different coloured threads are used; or it can also be used to fulfil a function. Using threads only will not allow any 'give' to the shirring, whereas if you use a narrow shirring elastic it will. The elastic is wound on the bobbin and a sewing thread is placed in the needle. When machining fabric this will give an automatic shirred effect, which will stretch as far as the elastic will. This is a good method for finishing any edge or section which is to be of adjustable size, eg, cuffs, neck, waist, pockets.

Method: Threads only.
This is the same as for machine or hand gathering except that several rows of stitching are done parallel to each other and of equal distance apart, before being pulled up. Do not remove the threads.

Figure 126

Elastic shirring

Shirring elastic is wound on to the bobbin so that it is stretched to its maximum. The machining is done as for above using a straight stitch. Several rows are stitched and great care must be taken to secure the ends.

Shirring elastic can also be stitched on fabric without being wound on bobbin (as can ordinary elastic). For this method however it is necessary to have a swing needle machine.

Method
This is worked over one thickness only except for any neatened edges, eg, hems.

1 Set machine to a zig-zag wide enough to take elastic comfortably and long enough to work easily.

2 Place fabric on machine ws up, place shirring elastic on top, underneath presser foot. Some machines have a special cording foot to hold cord or shirring elastic in place whilst working (if using these elastic will go between needle and fabric). Keeping elastic to the right position, pull taut with left hand while machining and use right hand to guide fabric.

3 Zig-zag over elastic to end. Repeat as often as required (fig 127).

Easing

Definition: Where a larger section of material is to be joined to a smaller section but is not big enough to take gathers, it is 'eased' or pushed into the right size on the fitting line. No gathers will form but the join will have a slightly rounded look on the right side of the larger section. Easing is done mainly when applying sleeve heads, bodice to yoke sections, collars and crossway.

Method

1 Mark off section to be eased.

2 Run two lines of running stitches or machine gathering stitches between these points. One on fitting line and one slightly above it (fig 128).

3 Pull up threads so that section is right size and pin to other garment sections. Push threads of gathered section well together on fitting line so that when sections are joined no pleats or gathers form on RS.

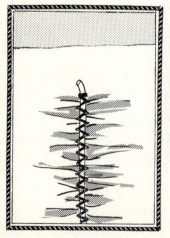

Figure 127

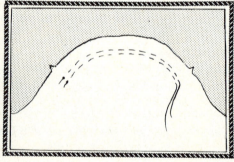

Figure 128

4 Tack and machine on fitting line. Remove tacks and gathers. Press well, pushing point of iron into eased part of join.

Golden rules for reduction of fullness
1 Always fit pattern accurately so any necessary adjustments can be made before cutting out. This is especially important when working out measurements for pleats.
2 Mark sections to be adjusted very clearly. (For marking see chapter 5.)
3 Check that sections to be reduced, in size or width, fit measurements of body or section they are to be joined to, *after* tacking and *before* machining.
4 Use a silk or fine thread, eg, Coats' Drima to hold pleats etc in place and do not remove until after garment has had its final press.
5 Choose right method of reduction for garment section and for fabric, eg, easing for sleeve heads, darts for body contouring. Tucks and gathers for fine to medium weight fabrics, and pleats for all types of fabric.
6 Take size and shape of person into account when choosing a method of reducing fullness, eg, gathers give a look of fullness where folds come – ideal for blouse fronts on small-breasted girls, terrible for the more well-endowed!

Words and terms used in this chapter (see Glossary for meanings)
Sewing terms

crossway	sleeve head	yoke
fitting line	tailor's tacks	zig-zag
fraying		

General terms

adjustable	encounter	parallel
angular	estimate	permutation
bulky	function	taper(ed)
comparatively	horizontal	techniques
contour	incorporate	vertical
distributed		

Things to do
1 List the places where you would use darts.
2 Give at least four places where you could use tucks and state why.
3 List six places where you could use gathers.
4 List four kinds of pleat and design a garment or two to incorporate two of the different kinds.

12. Seams

Definition: A seam is a line of stitching joining together two or more pieces of material.

Seams are important because 1 they hold sections of a garment together and 2 they give shape and emphasis to the line of the garment (fig 129).

Clothes which are tightly fitting are likely to have more seams and general shaping than those which are loose; for instance, a low-cut evening dress could need more seams than a smock top, to ensure that it curved to the body and did not gape. Some seams can be decorative as well as functional, eg, Piped and Channel seams (see pages 136 and 134).

Seams can be divided into two groups:

1 *Inconspicuous*: This means that the seam is not easily seen from the right side and there is no attention drawn to it by decorative features. Examples include open or plain seams.

Figure 129

2 *Conspicuous*: This refers to seams which have stitching showing on the right side. Sometimes this stitching is done to give extra strength as well as for decoration, eg, a double-stitched seam.

There are four main seams which are used in needlework; any others are really variations of the same or similar processes. These four seams are:
1 Open seam (also known as Flat or Plain seam).
2 French seam.
3 Overlaid (also known as Lapped or Top-stitched).
4 Double-stitched (also known as Run and Fell, and Machine Fell seam).

Instructions for making these seams are given later in this chapter.

A seam should be chosen for the job it must do. A strong seam such as a double-stitched one should be used where the garment must take the most strain, eg, the inner leg of jeans, or where there is frequent laundering, eg, on shirts.

Another factor to be taken into account when choosing a type of seam, is the fabric used. French seams, for instance, are ideal for fine, easily frayed material, but are not suitable for heavy, thick fabrics such as wool tweed (in the latter case the seam would be too bulky).

There are two technical terms which you will often encounter when reading about seams (especially in commercial patterns) and it will help you if you know what these mean.

The seam allowance or seam turning
This is the amount of fabric allowed from the pattern or fitting line to make the seam (fig 130). Most commercial patterns allow 1·5 cm but this may not always be sufficient for some fabrics or types of seam, so remember to allow extra if necessary at the cutting out stage.

The seam width
This is the final width of the seam when it is finished and may vary according to the type of seam and material used. This width is called the 'fell' in French and Double-stitched seams.

OPEN, FLAT OR PLAIN SEAM
This is the most commonly used of all seams. Made on the ws of the garment, it is inconspicuous and is used for joins which are meant to show very little, eg, shoulder and sleeve seams. The turnings of these seams may be pressed open, or flat to one side.

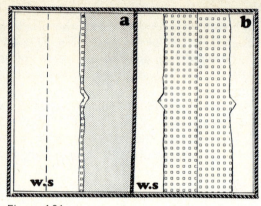

Figure 130

Figure 131

If the seams are to be edge-finished with a machine zig-zag stitch, you will find it easier to do this before joining the sections together, while the pieces are still lying flat. If you do this it may be necessary to trim the *seam allowance* parallel to the fitting line along the whole length of the seam. Zig-zagging edges before making up garment helps to prevent the fabric fraying. The garment should have been tacked together and fitted before edge-finishing because alterations afterwards will mean a seam allowance which looks like a switchback! This may not seem important as the seam will not be seen from the outside, but unevenness in the seam allowance can cause a garment to hang badly due to the uneven weight distribution (especially on very fine or soft draping fabrics).

Method for an open seam
1 Place two sections of garment to be joined RS together.
2 Pin along fitting line, first at balance marks then along whole length, placing pins at right angles to edge.
3 Tack over pins on fitting line (tacking can be omitted, following the method described in chapter 6, Helpful Hints).
4 Machine along fitting line (fig 131a).
5 Remove tacks, pins, press seam open (fig 131b) and finish raw edges by one of the neatening methods given in chapter 18, Seam Finishes.

FRENCH SEAM
This is usually classed as an inconspicuous, flat seam because it will not show on RS of the garment.

It is used on sheer or easily frayed materials and on clothes which will be washed a great deal such as blouses and underwear.

The raw edges are completely enclosed in the fell so do not need to be neatened. The width of the fell is decided by the choice of material – the firmer the material the *narrower* the fell; the more frayable the material the *wider* the fell. The finished width usually suitable for fine to medium weight fabrics is 0·5 cm.

Method for French seams

1 After tacking ws together trim seam allowance down to twice width of finished fell, eg, 1 cm allowance for 0·5 cm fell (fig 132a).

2 Remove pins and machine *above* the fitting line the width of the fell, eg, 0·5 cm finished fell means machining 0·5 cm above fitting line (fig 132b).

3 Trim seam allowance to slightly less than width of finished fell (eg, less than 0·5 cm for finished fell 0·5 cm) so the edges will be completely enclosed after machining (fig 132b).

4 Clip turnings on all curved edges almost to stitching line.

5 Remove tacking. Press seam open.

6 Turn to ws and press seam together (fig 132c).

7 Pin and tack on fitting line.

8 Remove pins, machine on fitting line (fig 132c).

9 Remove tacks, press seam fell to one side.

OVERLAID OR LAPPED SEAM

This is a conspicuous, flat seam which is both strong and decorative.

Figure 132

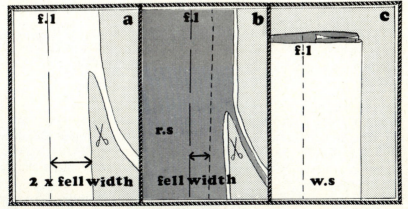

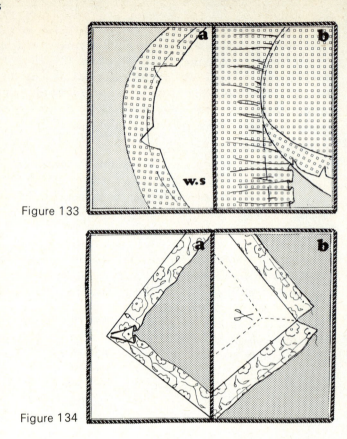

Figure 133

Figure 134

It is stitched through three thicknesses of material and is often used to join bodice sections together, or one shaped section to another, eg, a shaped yoke to a gathered bodice. The most important part of the process is to decide which piece of the garment is to be overlaid on to the other. The general rule is: a yoke section is overlaid on to the bodice; the centre panel of a skirt is overlaid on to the side panels; a plain section is overlaid on to one which has fullness.

Method for an overlaid seam
1 Mark fitting lines on each section (this is absolutely necessary).
2 Turn back seam allowance of *overlaying* section to ws. Pin and tack in place. Clip curves. Press turning on ws (fig 133a).
3 Gather up under section to required fullness or make darts, pleats, tucks, etc.
4 Place upper on to lower section, matching fold of upper to fitting

line of lower. Pin and tack in position, making sure that balance marks are matched on both pieces. This is necessary for a good fit and 'hang' to the garment (fig 133b).

5 Machine from 0·3 cm to 0·5 cm at an even distance from edge of fold on RS of garment. The smaller the article, the closer the machining should be to the fold, eg, on a baby's dress machine 0·3 cm from fold (fig 133b).

6 Neaten raw edges inside.

Coping with angles on overlaid seams
Outer angles: Pin and tack along one side. Trim surplus material on corner of second side before tacking down mitre (fig 134a).
Inner angles: Snip into angle diagonally before tacking down (fig 134b).

DOUBLE-STITCHED OR RUN AND FELL SEAMS
This is a very flat, conspicuous seam and is the strongest of all seams. The raw edges are completely enclosed, so do not need to be neatened, and it is easy to launder. It can be made on all except the bulkiest of fabrics. The seam can be made on to the RS or the WS of the garment but is easier to make on to the WS. In this instance only *one* row of stitching will show from the RS. It is more decorative to make the seam on to the RS of the garment as *two* rows of stitching will show. The width of the fell on this seam can vary from 0·3 cm to 1·5 cm with the narrower fell being used on fine fabrics.

Method for a double-stitched seam
1 Lay two sections of garment together (RS in, if seam is to be made on to WS; WS in, if seam is to be made on to RS, ie, showing).
2 Pin together vertically, first at balance points, then along whole length.
3 Tack and machine on fitting line (fig 135a). Remove pins.
4 Trim surplus material of one edge of seam allowance down to 0·5 cm (or half the fell width from line of machining) (fig 135a).
5 Remove tacks.
6 Trim surplus from other edge of seam allowance down to 1 cm from machine line (or twice width of finished fell) (fig 135a).
7 Fold and press larger edge over smaller (fig 135b).
8 Open two sections of garment and press down folded edge of seam on to garment so that it makes a flat join (enclosing all raw edges). Tack through three thicknesses of fabric close to fold. Machine on tacks (fig 135c). Remove tacks, press well from WS.

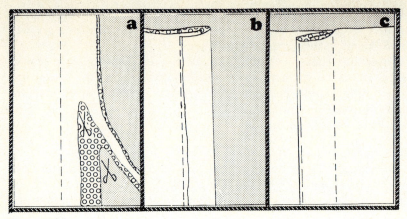

Figure 135

Variations of main seams

DOUBLE TOP STITCHED

This is a variation of the open or plain seam with the addition of a row of stitching either side of the main seam line at an even distance from it (fig 136).

CHANNEL SEAM

A channel seam is essentially a mixture of an open seam and a double top stitched seam, with the addition of a third layer of fabric between the join. The finished seam width is the distance between the two rows of top stitching.

Method for channel seam
1 Mark fitting lines on both sections to be joined.
2 Trim seam allowances evenly (parallel to fitting line), approximately 1·5 cm for finished channel width of 1·5 cm.
3 Fold back each section to fitting line. Tack and press to WS (fig 137a).
4 Cut a length of fabric on straight grain (see chapter 5) approximately 1·5 cm *wider* than finished seam width, and exact length of seam, eg, finished seam width 2·5 cm × seam length $\frac{1}{2}$ m, will need a strip of fabric 4 cm wide × $\frac{1}{2}$ m long.
5 Mark a line of tacking down centre of strip, along whole length.
6 Place strip RS up and position two garment sections on to this with *their* RS up, matching folded eges of each to centre line of lower strip (fig 137b).

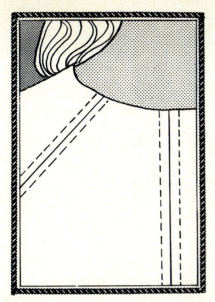

Figure 136

7 Pin and tack each piece into position. Remove pins; machine 0·5 cm from folded edge on each section through all thicknesses of material. This will give a 1·5 cm finished seam width (fig 137c).
8 Remove tacks, neaten inside raw edges and press on ws.

Extra emphasis can be gained by using different coloured fabric under the main fabric, giving a 'lightning flash' effect.

Figure 137

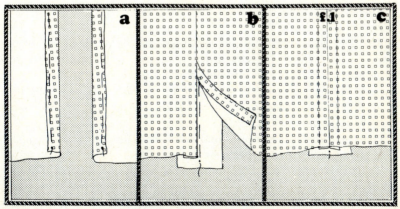

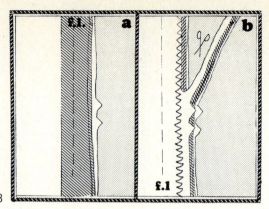

Figure 138

FLAT, PIPED OR CORDED, PIPED SEAMS

The addition of piping or corded piping will give a decorative finish to a seam. Coloured seam piping can be obtained from the haberdashery department of most large stores, or you can make up your own to match or contrast with the main fabric of the garment.

Method for a piped seam

1 Measure length of seam. Cut a length of piping fabric on the cross, slightly longer than length of seam (see chapter 8, Crossway). It should be twice width of finished piping, plus seam allowances, eg, 0·5 cm finished piping for a 10 cm long seam will require a strip of crossway approximately 4 cm × 11 cm (4 cm = 0·5 cm piping depth, 1·5 cm seam allowance).

2 Mark fitting lines on both sections of garment to be joined.

3 Fold crossway strip in half lengthways (ws together). Tack through both thicknesses 0·5 cm from fold (for a 0·5 cm deep piping).

4 Position piping on RS of one section of garment, matching fitting lines on garment to tacking lines on piping. Be sure to point fold of piping *away* from raw edge of garment section (fig 138a).

5 Place second section of garment on to first with RS together, matching fitting lines and balance points. Pin and tack on fitting line through all thicknesses.

6 Remove pins and machine on fitting line (fig 138b).

7 Remove tacks, press seam open.

8 Trim raw edges to same depth and neaten all layers together using zig-zag (fig 138b).

For this seam to look good, the piping must be of an even width along the seam, therefore tacking is a very important part of the process.

For both a flat, piped and a corded, piped seam it is easier to use a zipper foot attachment on the machine when working. The needle position is altered to the right or left according to where the piping is placed.

Corded, piped seam construction
Identical to a flat, piped seam, but cording is inserted into crossway strip before tacking down and before insertion into seam.

Do not pipe seams which are likely to chafe the skin, eg, armholes, or legs of baby clothes.

For joins and angles in piping see chapter 21, Pipings.

QUICK FRENCH SEAM
This seam is suitable for firm, fine to medium weight fabrics. It is both quick to make and neat and efficient in wear.

Method
1 Make up seam as for open or plain seam to end of stage **4**.
2 Set machine to a suitable zig-zag for the fabric (practise on spare fabric).
3 Using edge of presser foot as a guide (keep left edge parallel with first row of machining), stitch whole length of seam with zig-zag.

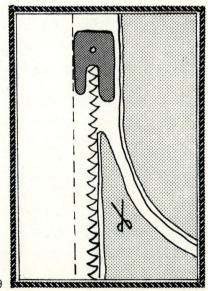

Figure 139

4 Trim surplus seam allowance down to zig-zag being careful not to cut into stitching. Press seam flat to one side (fig 139).

Golden rules for seams
1 Fit garment first before trimming any seam allowances.
2 Mark fitting lines clearly using tacking or trace marks.
3 Pin or tack seams together carefully, before machining.
4 Machine *slowly* if you tend to get wiggly seams. It does not matter if you seem to be taking a long time. Remember the tortoise and the hare?
5 Where possible neaten edges of seams *before* joining sections together.
6 Use correct tension and stitch length to avoid puckering of seams.
7 Use right thread for fabric, eg, Coats' Drima (see Golden Rules, chapter 7).
8 Choose right seam for work it must do, eg, a strong seam for garments which must take a lot of wear; a flat seam for easy laundering and extra comfort if garment is worn next to body.
9 Press seams carefully *before* joining next section. Pressing seams as you go will give your work a professional finish (see chapter 24, Pressing).
10 Allow enough seam allowance for type of seam and fabric used. Allow extra for easily frayed materials.
11 Neaten raw edges to give clothes a longer life.

Words and terms used in this chapter (see Glossary for meanings)
Sewing terms
seams: open, flat, plain   overlaid, lapped
        channel   French, quick French
        corded   piped
        double stitched, machine fell, run and fell
        double top stitched

balance points	fitting lines	seam width
bodice	overcasting	sheer
cord(ing)	piping	yoke
fell	seam allowance	

General terms

bulky	emphasis	surplus
conspicuous	fray(able)	tension
commercial	inconspicuous	variation
distribution	parallel	vertical

Things to do
1 List at least four kinds of seams and state where you would use each type.
2 On what kind of fabrics would you use a French seam? For what kind of fabrics would you use an overlaid seam?
3 What kind of seams would you use on a thick woollen coat? Describe and give reasons for choice.
4 Make up samples of each kind of seam using an assortment of fabrics. Note stitch length and tension used.

◎　◎　◎

13.　Openings

Openings on a garment must allow easy access to the body and, when they are fastened, the garments should fit well in the right places. Openings and fastenings are the two halves of a process which allows this.

There are, however, various kinds of openings and just as many kinds of fastenings. The choice of each will depend on a number of factors, such as the fabric used and the position on the garment. Remember that any opening (especially on close fitting garments) will take more strain and wear than any other part, so it needs to be strongly made and have strong fastenings.

There are two main types of opening, each type having variations. The two types are those with a *wrap* and those without.

◎　WRAP OPENINGS　◎

Definition: An opening in a garment made and finished so that the two edges of the opening overlap; the overlap and underlap together making the *wrap*.

CONTINUOUS WRAP OPENING
This is also known as a continuous strip opening and can be used on:
1 Sleeves at the cuff.
2 Sometimes at side openings of skirts and trousers.
3 Neck openings of shirts, dresses, etc.

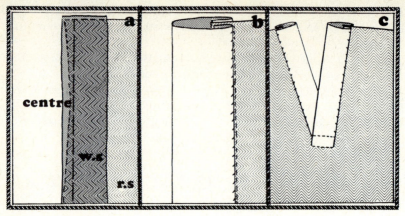

Figure 140

It is suitable for fine to medium weight fabrics only, because of the number of layers of fabric which make the wrap; these would make it too bulky if using a heavy material.

Method for an opening into a slit
1 Cut strip of fabric on straight grain (see chapter 5) twice length of opening, and twice width of finished wrap plus 1 cm; eg, for a finished opening 7 cm × 1·5 cm, cut a strip 14 cm × 4 cm.
2 Press under 0·5 cm turning to wrong side along one edge of strip. Tack into place.
3 Lay raw edge of strip to raw edge of opening, RS together. Pin and tack into place using small stitches and being careful at the turn.
4 Hold opening so raw edges of each side form a straight line. Machine 0·5 cm from raw edge making sure no fabric is caught or puckered in the process (tapering centre of strip) (fig 140a).
5 Remove tacks and press. Turn the wrap (strip) to ws, enclosing all raw edges (fig 140b).
6 Tack down to machine stitching and hem into place (as described in chapter 7, Hand Stitches), so no stitches show on RS.
7 Remove tacks. Decide which part of wrap is to be underneath. Fold and press under.
8 For extra strength, machine across base of opening in a box shape (fig 140c).
9 If opening is to look neat and take much wear, overlap edge can be machined along edges so it lies flat.

Method for wrap opening made into a seam
Almost the same process as for a slit opening with a wrap.
1 Join seam as far as beginning of opening.
2 Trim excess fabric from seam allowance. Snip across turning and finish off raw edges (fig 141).
2 Make strip and continue through stages 1–8 as for slit opening. It is unnecessary to taper the opening at garment edge.

HEM OPENINGS
These also have a wrap which can be self-made or false (facing type) if there is not enough material. A hem opening is the strongest of all openings and is used for clothing and household articles which take a lot of strain, eg, shirt fronts, loose cushion covers, etc. They are usually made into a seam or through the whole length of a garment, eg, a button-through skirt (fig 142).

Definition: A hem (false or self-made) is formed on both edges and the two hems overlapped.

Method
1 Decide on type of fastening and make hem allowance (or seam allowance) of article big enough to take this, eg, a 1·5 cm button will need a hem at least 2 cm wide, so allow extra material.

Figure 142

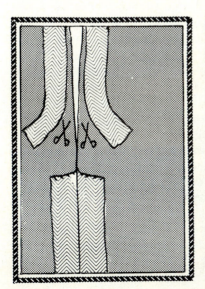

2 Secure hems into position (see chapter 23, Hems). On blouses and skirts, only machine first turning of hem. Second turning is left free except where it is fixed by fastenings.

(For false hems, also see chapter 23.)

◎ OPENINGS WITHOUT A WRAP ◎

Definition: Any opening where the two edges just meet without any overlap, sometimes known as slit openings. These openings (with the exception of zipped openings) are not so strong as openings with a wrap.

FACED SLIT OPENINGS

Often used at necks of blouses and dresses or sleeve openings. Suitable for all except the most transparent materials (the facing would show through on RS). Neck facings are sometimes cut as one with the facing for the opening.

The facing is usually made on to the WS of the garment and is therefore inconspicuous but of course can be made on to the RS as a design feature. (For more information on facings see chapter 19, Facings.)

Method for an inconspicuous faced opening
1 Mark position of opening on garment with a line of tacking.
2 If there is no pattern piece for facing, cut a strip of fabric on the straight grain (see chapter 5) the length of opening, plus 5 cm, and at least 7 cm wide (it can be narrower for very fine cottons etc on short openings).
3 Fold a 0·5 cm turning allowance under on to WS of facing, along two long and one short sides. Tack and machine into place. For a less bulky facing on firm fabrics, do not turn under but neaten raw edges of three sides with a close zig-zag stitch.
4 Mark line of tacking on facing the exact length of opening, starting from centre of raw edge and keeping line in centre all the way along.
5 Place RS of facing to RS of garment, matching tacking lines of both pieces. Baste into position (see chapter 7, Hand Stitches) (fig 143a).
6 Remove pins and machine 0·3 cm each side of tacks, tapering to a point at base of opening. Cut along marked opening almost to machining at base point (fig 143b).
7 Remove tacks and basting stitches. Press, turn through to WS,

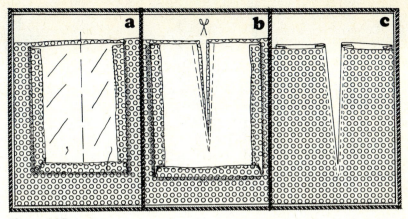

Figure 143

keeping seam edge crisp. Press again. If facing is to be left free, machine very close to opening edge all around to hold in place (fig 143c).

CONSPICUOUS SLIT OPENING
Same method as for inconspicuous faced opening with some differences.
1 Facing can be shaped at base of opening if wished.
2 It is unnecessary to machine turning down on facing. Tack only.
3 Place RS of facing to WS of garment.
4 After turning facing through finish with line of machining all around outer edge to hold in position (fig 144).

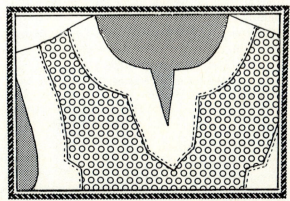

Figure 144

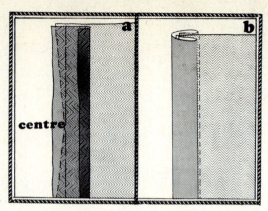

Figure 145

BOUND OPENING

Suitable for finer materials, eg, cottons, rayons, etc. (See also chapter 20, Bindings.)

Method for bound openings

1 Mark opening in garment and cut through length.

2 Cut crossway strip twice length of opening × 4 times width of finished bind, eg, an opening 10 cm long with a 0·5 cm bind will need a strip 20 cm long × 2 cm wide. (See cutting and joining crossway strips, chapter 8, Crossway.) A commercial binding can be used on certain garments, eg, nightwear, pinafores and smocks for children.

3 Turn each raw edge of strip lengthways to centre (ws together). Press lightly. Fold strip in half lengthways (ws in). Press again.

4 Open out binding and place on to opening, RS and raw edges together. Pin and tack along crease line tapering edge of opening towards centre on garment side only, as for continuous strip opening (fig 145a).

5 Remove pins, machine along tacking. Remove tacks, press.

6 Fold bind on to ws and hem into place just above machine line (fig 145b).

For Golden Rules etc see end of chapter 14.

14. Fastenings

Definition: Any method which holds together opposite parts of garments or articles.

Fastenings can cover any method for holding together neck, back and front, sleeve edges, etc, from laces and eyelets, buttons and buttonholes, to safety pins! There are so many types of fastening that a beginner might be bewildered by the choice. One of the most popular types of fastening for the home dressmaker, because of its easy application, is the zip fastener.

The zip fastener
A zip fastening is the part of a zipped opening which holds the two edges of the opening together. It is usually one of the strongest methods of fastening and is easy to launder and press, although special care must be taken with Nylon zips. Zips can be used almost anywhere on a garment; neck, back, front and all kinds of openings on dresses, trousers and skirts; front openings of coats and jackets; sleeves and pockets; cushion covers and bags, etc.

Zips come in various colours, weights and lengths, eg, Nylon zips for the opening of synthetic fibre clothes; special invisible zips for skirts and dresses (giving a concealed finish to the opening); open-ended zips for cardigans and jackets; curved zips for trouser front openings and chunky fashion zips which are meant to show as part of the design.

Zips can be inserted in two ways:

1 *Into a slit opening*: In this instance the teeth will show, so the method is only suitable for certain purposes.

2 *Into a seam*: Either by concealed or semi-concealed method.

When machining zips try to use a zipper foot attachment on the machine. This has only one side to the foot and the needle position can be altered on the machine to go into the side which is free. This makes the application of zips (especially over the tag part of the zip) much easier.

Method for setting zip into slit opening
1 Mark opening on garment with line of tacking. Length of opening will be measured from fitting line down. Zip length should be

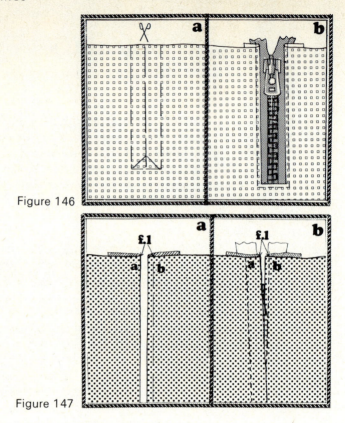

Figure 146

Figure 147

length of opening from fitting line to base, less about 1·5 cm.

2 Measure slide of zip at widest part and tack round opening the same width (equal distance from first row of tacking and straight across base). Base can be strengthened with extra fabric at this stage if wished (fig 146a).

3 Cut into opening following first line of tacks until 0·5 cm from base, then snip across diagonally to each corner (fig 146a).

4 Fold back turnings on WS to second row of tacking all round. Pin and tack down. Remove pins. Press lightly. Turn to RS.

5 Position zip under opening slide upwards and 1·5 cm from top fitting line, making it evenly placed all the way down. Pin and tack down (fig 146b).

6 Remove pins and slide zip up and down to make sure it moves freely, then machine 0·3 cm from edge all round (fig 146b).

For extra strength on bags, cases, upholstery, etc, machine again over first line of stitches.

CONCEALED ZIPS

Definition: The zip cannot be seen from RS, but a row of stitching shows along one side.

Often used for side, front or back openings, especially where there might be strain on the opening which could cause gaping.

Method
1 Join seam of garment to bottom of opening. Press open seam and press seam turning under, to fitting line, on one side of opening (side **a**).
2 Press other seam turning under, almost to fitting line. Leave about 0·3 cm extra all the way down (side **b**) (fig 147a).
3 Position zip 1·5 cm from top fitting line (or at *top* of opening if zip is set into side opening of dress etc). Place one side of row of teeth almost to fold of side **b**. Pin and tack close to edge all way down (fig 147b).
4 Lay side **a** over zip. Pin and tack in place along side and bottom just far enough from folded edge to clear teeth (fig 147b).
5 Remove pins and check that zipper moves freely along its length. Machine along tacks. Remove tacks. Press.

SEMI-CONCEALED ZIP

Definition: The zip is inserted into an opening with the edges just meeting and is held in place by a row of stitching of even distance all the way round.

Because the zipper teeth may show slightly during wear, this method is only suitable for some purposes, eg, openings at the neck of loose garments, sleeve openings, pockets, etc.

Method
1 Join seam to base of opening. Press open and press under seam allowances to fitting line on both sides. Tack down.
2 Position zip 1·5 cm from top fitting line (or level with fitting line for closed top openings). Pin and tack evenly into place along length and across end as close to teeth as possible, but allowing zipper free movement (fig 148).
3 Remove pins, check zip moves freely. Machine on tacking line. Remove tacks, press.

'INVISIBLE' ZIP

This type of zip looks like a seam. Follow the maker's instructions for attaching.

Figure 148   Figure 149

Other fastenings

Apart from zip fasteners, other types of fastening may be equally suitable for the garment you are making; some types are easier to make than others.

Cost should also be taken into consideration, eg, rouleaux or ribbon ties are a cheap way of fastening clothes. The following methods and suggestions are for fastenings and their possible uses, but you may be able to think up some ideas of your own which will give your clothes a really original look.

BUTTONS

Buttons and methods of fastening them have been used for many centuries, but fortunately for us we no longer have to fumble with dozens of tiny buttons at blouse front or cuff, as the modern zipper and elastic have done away with that drudgery. However, we do still have a need for buttons, on shirts, jackets, coat and dress fronts, cuffs, neck edges, even trouser flies, although buttons are fewer on a garment than they used to be. Buttons can also hold down pockets and tabs, or hold a belt or collar in place. The methods of fastening a button can be as follows: piped, bound, machine or hand-worked buttonholes; and rouleaux, ribbon, braid or hand-worked buttonloops.

Points to remember when making fastenings using buttons
1 If the opening is edge to edge, buttons can only be used with *loops* to fasten. After making the garment, mark the positions of the buttons and work hand-made loops to match. Or, for rouleaux and braid loops, insert these first in the edge facing before making the garment, then match the buttons later.
2 For overlapping edges, first decide whether the buttonholes are to be vertical or horizontal (often vertical on front dress edges but should be horizontal for efficiency). Mark buttonholes on garment and make them large enough to take buttons comfortably without being loose.
3 Horizontal buttonholes should have the *round* edge nearest to the *outer* edge of the opening and be half the width of the button, from the edge, eg, for a 2 cm wide button, hole should have its rounded end placed 1 cm from edge of opening or on CF (fig 149).
  For safety when cutting buttonholes, put pin in middle and cut from each end towards pin with a stitch ripper. This will avoid accidental ripping.

BOUND BUTTONHOLES
Bound buttonholes are not suitable for clothes which are frequently washed, as they are not very strong and the extra wear from laundering could cause fraying. However they are suitable for woollen coats and jackets, or outer garments which have to be dry cleaned.
  Buttonholes can be bound in a contrasting colour to the main garment, or they can be of a different material, giving a contrast in texture. This may be necessary if the material of the garment is very thick. The usual depth of the bind is from 0·3 cm to 0·5 cm. The measurement for the binding piece should be:
Width: Half the diameter of the button plus 2·5 cm.
Length: At least 5 cm or always 2·5 cm longer than the width.
  Therefore a 2 cm wide button needs a binding piece 3·5 cm × 6 cm.
  For firmness and extra strength tack a small piece of backing fabric or fine interfacing to inside of garment piece before making up.

Method
1 Mark buttonhole position and length on garment with tacks.
2 Lay binding strip over mark on RS of work, keeping centre of strip to centre of buttonhole. Pin and tack.

3 Remove pins. Machine a rectangle around line of tacking (fig 150a).

4 Cut along centre of buttonhole on tacking line almost to each end. Snip diagonally into corners (fig 150a).

5 Press back turnings and two triangular ends (fig 150b).

6 Pull strip through to ws making sure all raw edges are enclosed and strip is lying flat. Each end will make a small inverted pleat (fig 150c). Tack opening.

7 Remove pins. Turn to RS of work, then using backstitch (see chapter 7, Hand Stitches) work through all thicknesses along two long seams (fig 150d).

8 Fold back fabric so triangles show, and backstitch across and through pleat (fig 150e).

Figure 150

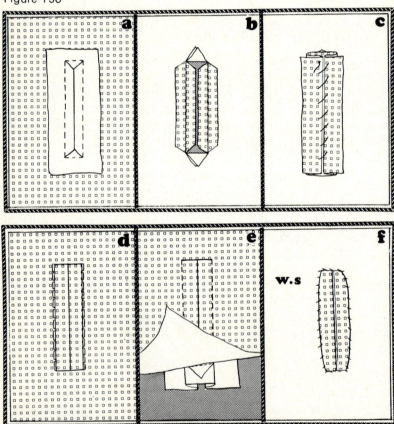

9 After putting on facing, mark positions of buttonholes by putting pin in each end through all thicknesses. Mark off with chalk on facing, a line between the two pins. Remove pins and slit facing on line almost to each end, snip diagonally into corners.

10 Turn under facing and hem in place all round. Edges of facing should reach outer bound edge of buttonhole. Do not stitch too tightly or buttonhole will pucker (fig 150f).

PIPED BUTTONHOLES

These look very smart on a garment, giving a professional finish which is both strong and decorative. They are easy to make.

Piped buttonholes vary from bound buttonholes in that they are formed from *two* pieces of material instead of one, and the material can be cut on the cross *or* the straight grain.

Method for piped buttonholes

1 Mark position and size of buttonholes on garment with tacks.

2 Cut a strip of fabric 2·5 cm wide × four times the length of buttonhole. Fold strip in half along its length, ws inside. Tack and machine 0·3 cm from folded edge (fig 151a).

3 Trim edges to 0·3 cm from machine line then remove tacks. Cut strip in half to make *two* strips each twice the length of finished buttonhole.

4 Position strips over buttonhole on RS of garment so raw edges of strip are facing together and are even with the buttonhole markings. Tack and machine along piping strip following first line of machining (ie, 0·3 cm from fold edge), keeping stitching to same length as finished buttonhole (fig 151b).

5 From ws of garment, cut along buttonhole markings and into corners up to line of machining (fig 151c).

6 Turn strips through to ws so that folded edges are now together giving a neat finish on RS of garment. Press well.

7 Fold back strip to show triangular ends and stitch across these a few times to secure (fig 151d).

8 Hand sew facing strip in place over back of buttonhole, pressing on ws with damp cloth.

WORKED BUTTONHOLES

A HAND-MADE

There are three kinds of hand-made buttonholes:

1 *Two round ends*: Used as a casing opening for elastic and belts. Usually made on single material.

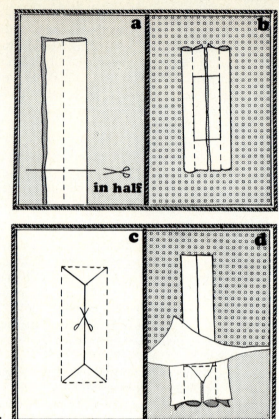

Figure 151

2 *Two square ends*: Used for vertical buttonholes where there is not much strain or if strain is downwards, eg, dress fronts.

3 *One round end and one square end*: Used for horizontal button-holes where strain is taken across buttonhole. The rounded end holds shank of button so will always be placed to outside edge of garment.

Method
1 Mark positions of buttonholes on RS.
2 Machine 0·2 cm from mark all round and straight across ends. Cut through marks.
3 Beginning at left hand lower corner, work line of buttonhole stitches (see chapter 7) to other end, just outside line of machining. Use Coats' Drima for medium weight fabrics and Coats' Bold Stitch for heavier weight fabrics.

4 For round end, overcast 5 or 7 times spreading stitches to a fan shape.

5 Continue along second edge using buttonhole stitch. Make two or three long stitches to form a square end (fig 152a).

6 Work buttonhole stitch across this bar to make a firm end (fig 152a).

Buttonholes with two *square* ends will have stage **6** repeated at each end (fig 152b).

Buttonholes with two *round* ends will have stage **4** repeated at each end (fig 152c).

B MACHINE-MADE BUTTONHOLES

Some fully automatic machines will make buttonholes at the twist of a dial. However, with a little care, ordinary swing needle machines will also make strong buttonholes. They are quick and easy to do, but take your time at first. Practise on spare fabric before you begin.

Method

1 Decide on length of buttonholes and mark on garment with chalk or tacks.

2 Set machine to zig-zag suitable for buttonhole (length 0·2–0·5 cm according to machine, fabric and thread used; width will vary according to the size of the buttonhole).

3 Beginning at far end of *left hand* side of buttonhole, machine slowly to near end. Be sure that needle meets line of tacks or marks

Figure 152

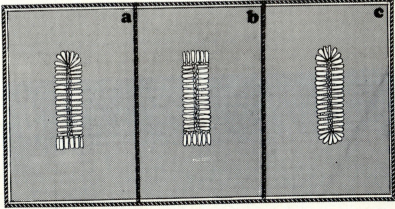

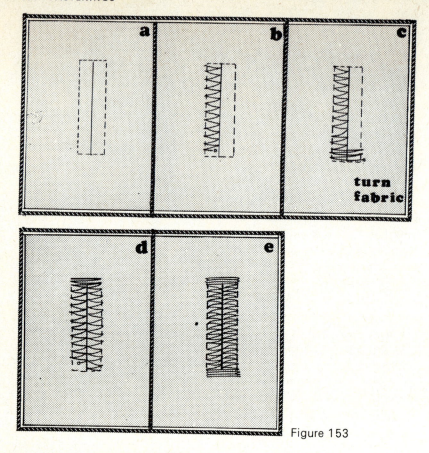

Figure 153

on *right hand* side of swing, and encloses row of machining on *left hand* side of swing (fig 153a).

4 At end, stop with needle in material at *left hand side* of zig-zag, then by hand turn wheel so needle is at its highest point. Stop.

5 Set stitch width dial to *twice* width it was, ie, if it was 2, set it to 4. Using hand control make three or four bar stitches, finishing with needle in fabric at *right hand side* of zig-zag (fig 153b).

6 Lift presser foot, and with needle still in fabric, swing garment round so that needle is now at *far end* of buttonhole. Put presser foot back down. Lift needle to its highest point. Set dials back to *half* width and machine slowly to end (fig 153c).

7 Repeat stages **5** and **6**, finishing with needle out of material (fig 153d).

8 To finish, set machine to straight stitch (width 0 – length 2) and work a couple of straight stitches manually, but holding fabric so that stitches are worked in one spot. Take all loose threads to back of work and sew in (fig 153e).

9 Cut through buttonhole carefully, from end to end.

BUTTONLOOPS

Usually made on edge of garment, but can be concealed by making on to overlap (on ws) some way on from edge.

Method
1 Join opening together and mark with pin where centre of each buttonloop will come (they should be of equal distance apart).
2 Mark (with tailor's tacks) beginning and end of each loop (equal distance from either side of pin). The space between should be same as diameter of button (fig 154a).
3 Remove pins. Starting at one tailor's tack, insert needle threaded with button thread and work a few backstitches to begin. Take thread over to other tack mark and work a few stitches. Take thread back to first mark. Repeat three or four times.

To make sure that loops are of an even size and right size for button, draw a line on a strip of paper or tape and place this under work so that marked line is parallel to edge of work and at half the width of button from it. Place a pin into paper so that it is centralized to the tailor's tack on garment, and first spearing of pin is on marked line on the paper. When bar stitches are worked, take them behind pin (fig 154a).
4 Remove paper and pins. Turn work and begin working loop. Buttonhole or blanket stitch can be used but make sure loops of

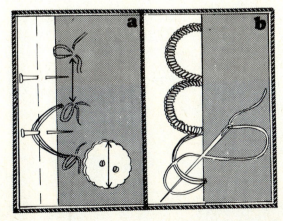

Figure 154

each stitch are at outer edge of buttonloop and that they are firm but not overcrowded. Work to end and finish with backstitches on WS of work (fig 154b).

BRAID AND RIBBON LOOPS

These can be made on the edge of the work after the garment is made up or they can be enclosed in the facing before making up. They are quick and easy to do.

Method

1 Measure button diameter and allow braid $1\frac{1}{4}$ times this measurement plus turnings (if it is to be a single loop).

2 Mark off position of loops with tacks and pins as for worked buttonloops, and position braid on opening edge, allowing extra for turning under and neatening at end of each loop or row of loops (if they are close together). If ribbon or braid is flat, for a neat finish, crease first diagonally at outer and inner points before securing (fig 155).

3 Pin and tack in place. On WS, either sew where edges meet, or, for a very quick method, on the RS slightly overlap garment fabric on to loops and machine stitch very close to edge where braid and garment join (fig 155).

BUTTONLOOPS LET INTO A FACING

1 Mark fitting line on garment.

2 Make up braid or ribbon loops to size, and position on RS, so outer edge of loop faces inner side of garment, ie, raw edges will face same side. Fitting lines or inner edges of loops should match

Figure 155   Figure 156

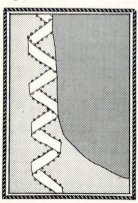
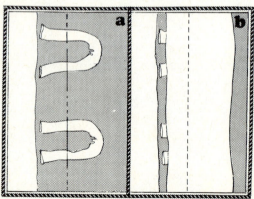

fitting line of garment. Pin and tack on fitting line (fig 156a).

3 Remove pins. Place facing on to garment, RS together, matching fitting lines, balance points, etc (fig 156b). Pin and tack on fitting line and open out. Check all loops are caught into garment and are of even size.

4 Remove pins. Machine on fitting line. Remove tacks. Layer seams. Clip curves. Fold facing on to WS and neaten raw edges. Press well.

ROULEAU BUTTONLOOPS

These are made from crossway fabric (see cutting and joining crossway, chapter 8) either of same or contrasting fabric to garment. Use same procedure for applying them as for ribbon and braid loops.

If there is a close row of loops, they can be applied after garment is made, in one long strip, measured to fit with each raw end neatened. Or they can be applied before facing is put on to garment, in which case one or more separate loops can be made as raw ends will not show.

Buttonloops of rouleau can be corded for extra emphasis (see chapter 8) but corded loops set into facings will cause extra bulk so are only suitable for fine fabrics.

SEWING ON BUTTONS

There are two kinds of buttons, those with a shank (a raised part underneath) and those without.

Shank buttons are preferable for outdoor garments because the shank will allow the button to move freely even if the material is very thick. Also, a shank made of plastic, wood or bone, is less likely to wear down than one made of threads. However, a shank should be made even on flat buttons, to allow ease of movement; it can be formed of thread.

Method for buttons without a shank

1 Mark position of button with a pin. The shank of the button should come close to the end of the buttonhole closest to opening edge, for horizontal buttonholes; centred for vertical ones (fig 157a).

2 Sew on double material using a strong buttonhole thread or linen thread, eg, Coats' Drima or Bold Stitch. Sew a few back-stitches to start, then work through one hole and across a matchstick to other; this leaves stitches loose enough to form a shank. Repeat until button feels secure, then remove matchstick (fig 157b).

3 Pull needle out until it is between fabric and button, slide button

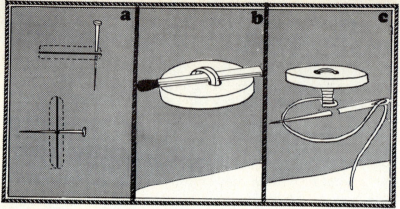

Figure 157

up threads as far as it will go, wind cotton in needle round threads so a shank is formed. Finish off firmly on ws (fig 157c).

PRESS STUDS AND FASTENERS

With the exception of heavy duty fasteners such as are found on jeans and some types of denim jackets, these are not really suitable for any opening where there is a lot of strain. There is a new type of gripper snap fastener which does not need sewing. These were originally used on denim shirts and stretch towelling jump suits for babies. They soon became popular for other garments as they can easily be applied with a special tool which will also make eyelets. However, great care must be taken to ensure the studs are positioned correctly, as once they are on it is difficult to remove them without damaging the material.

As well as metal, some press studs are made of transparent plastic or Nylon and these are perfect for underwear, nightclothes, or very delicate garments. They are also ideal for baby clothes as they will not dig into a baby's soft skin.

Method: For untextured fabrics (not woollen tweeds etc)
Rub knob part with tailor's chalk and press overlaying garment section on to underlay, matching fitting lines. Chalk mark will show on one side giving guideline to exact position to sew corresponding piece of stud.

HOOKS, EYES AND BARS

These are nearly always hidden except where they are a design feature, as with giant hooks and eyes (the type furriers use) found on some front fastenings. They often hold together openings which do not have any overlap but meet edge to edge, eg, slit openings and zipped openings.

They help to secure the opening on the points where there is the most strain (usually at the top of the opening).

Method for hook and eye
1 Hook is usually fixed behind right-hand side of opening, almost to edge on ws of work. Secure hook using oversewing stitches across bar, close to bend of hook; using oversewing or buttonhole stitches through loops, make sure that hook is held firm (fig 158).
2 Eye is sewn to other edge of opening on ws so it sticks out slightly from edge (necessary for hook to fasten properly). Oversew or buttonhole stitch round each loop (fig 158).

Hooks and bars are used on any opening where there is an overlap or wrap, eg, the waistband of a skirt. Sometimes bars are metal and sometimes handworked.

Method for handworked bars
1 Mark position of bar on garment.
2 Make three or four long stitches across this point, beginning with a few backstitches to secure. Buttonhole or loop stitch along bar, without catching up underneath fabric (fig 159).

'VELCRO'
This is the trade name for a special kind of fastening one side of which catches the other at a touch and opens when pulled apart

Figure 158

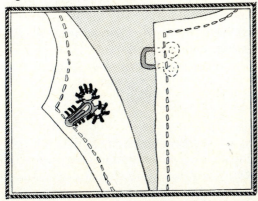

Figure 159

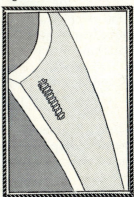

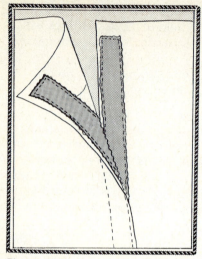

Figure 160

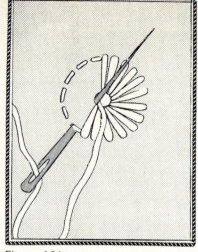

Figure 161

firmly. Very quick and easy to apply, it works because one side has a lot of hooks and the other side has a lot of loops. The contact of the two makes them interlock. It is fine for certain purposes, eg, Nylon, Terylene or plastic rainwear; bags and cases; nightwear and stage costumes – anywhere where a quick fastener is needed.

Method
1 Place hooked side to overlaying edge of garment on ws of work. Pin in place or stick down one edge with tape (the edge not being machined first).
2 Machine along the narrow plain strip at edge of 'Velcro', stitching the whole length. Machine across top, remove sticky tape, machine along other edge and along bottom. Repeat procedure with looped side, but placing it on RS of other garment section, matching fitting lines (fig 160).

Use large stitches on 'Velcro' for easier sewing, especially on Nylon, PVC or plastic rainwear. When washing, keep the two sections closed to prevent fluff causing difficulties when fastening.

Miscellaneous fastenings
Besides the previously mentioned fastenings, there are also ties, laces, eyelets, buckles, straps, frogs and so on, and with variations to each of these the number of possible types and styles is almost limitless.

EYELETS AND LACES

(For eyelets – use overcasting stitch and Coats' Drima.)
Ideal used where opening is to be of adjustable size. Can be an
attractive design feature too (fig 161, eyelets). Laces can be made of
ribbon, braid, rouleaux strips (see chapter 8) or coloured lacing of
all kinds. White shoelaces can be dyed any colour and are easy to
thread as they have ends which are secured in a metal clasp. For
wider ribbons and laces it is best to work double round-ended
buttonholes to fit (see page 155).

TIE STRINGS, BUCKLES AND STRAPS

Used for easily adjustable fastenings. Use plain or coloured tape
for household use – loose covers etc; use Nylon, satin or velvet
ribbon for children's clothes, underwear or nightwear; and for
outer garments such as jerkins, jackets, tie neck shirts, etc, use
leather, suede, wool braid, cotton tape, or self fabrics.

Buckle fastenings can be made on to tapes or tie strings, by the
same method as below except that of course the ties will be shorter,
eg, the leather type buckle fastenings on a pleated skirt or kilt. Some
buckles are stitched directly to the garment but they still need a
strap to link the two parts of the garment together.

Ties can be stitched to RS or WS of garments.

Methods for stitching on tapes, ties or buckle straps
1 Cut tape to required size plus turnings. On wrap openings tie
will be stitched to RS of underlapping edge and to WS of overlapping
edge.
2 Turn back one fold 0·3 cm wide on end (to WS) or two folds if
fabric frays easily; machine across once or twice to hold down.
3 Turn back a 1·5 cm turning to WS at other end of tape. Press
lightly and position on to garment. Machine in place using box
shape, and for extra strength machine diagonally into corners
(fig 162). Non-fray materials such as leather need not have turnings.

Method for buckles
1 Cut strip for eyelet end of strap and stitch on garment as given
for tapes. Eyelet end will be sewn to overlapping edge. Make eyelets
by hand first or attach metal eyelets with special tool, afterwards.
2 Cut strap for buckle. This should be twice length of finished strap
plus turnings. Slide buckle on to strap and pin to hold. Turn under
1·5 cm, then fold strap exactly in half widthways, sliding raw edges
of one half under turned edge of the other. Place on garment and
machine in place through all thicknesses (fig 163).

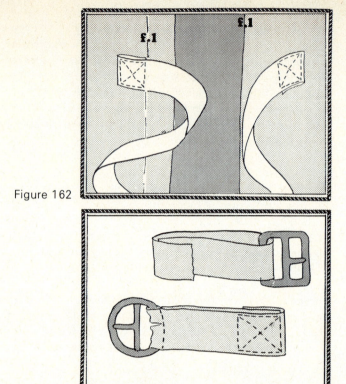

Figure 162

Figure 163

3 Stitch a line close to buckle through *tape only* to prevent it slipping up and down. Do this by hand using backstitch (see chapter 7) or by machine (keep clear of buckle).

Golden rules for openings and fastenings

1 Decide on types of openings and fastenings when buying pattern and before buying fabric. Some kinds of openings are more suitable than others for certain fabrics.

2 If choice is a zipped opening, try to buy zip at same time as fabric to get a good colour match. Make sure zip is the right kind for the job it must do, eg, metal, Nylon, open or closed ended, etc.

3 Mark openings and tack up garment for fitting. When fitting, make sure opening is big enough to allow easy entry and will close without straining.

4 Make up openings before applying facings etc (especially at neck edges).

5 Fastenings inserted into a facing are made up and applied before facing is put on.

6 For centre back zips, make up back seam as far as bottom of opening and apply zip before joining back section of garment to front sections. It is much easier this way.

7 Use a zipper foot attachment on machine where applicable, as this will allow a close machine line even across the wide part of a zip. The long metal foot goes along one side of the needle only, leaving the side next to the zip free.

Words and terms used in this chapter (see Glossary for meanings)
Sewing terms

clip curves	layer seams	synthetic
clip seam	seam allowance	tailor's tacks
fitting line	shank	zig-zag
interfacing	straight grain	

General terms

access	contrasting	inconspicuous
adjustable	corresponding	miscellaneous
application	diameter	parallel
approximately	diagonally	rectangle
centralized	factors	texture
commercial	function	variations
concealed	horizontal	vertical
conspicuous	identical	

Things to do
1 Make up three new fastenings; either draw them or make them as fabric samples. State where you might use them.
2 List six places where you might use zip fasteners. Be imaginative!

◎ ◎ ◎

15. Collars

Although some styles of clothing are collarless, nothing gives a garment a more distinctive touch than a well-made, well-set, collar. Even the plainest outfit can be brightened by the addition of a

Figure 164

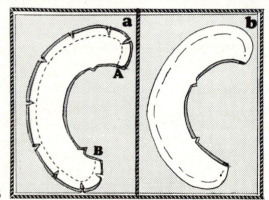

Figure 165

collar, perhaps in a contrasting colour or fabric.

Collars can be detachable, and can be made of a single or double thickness, of fabric. Often, however, it is attached to the garment in the process of making up and is made of double material, the pieces being known as the *upper* and *under* collar.

Collars are not the easiest part of a garment to apply and it really pays to take some time over the fitting, pinning and tacking stages, as nothing looks worse than a collar that has gone askew giving the wearer a lop-sided look, or one which is the wrong size.

There are two main types of collar:

1 *Flat*: This is like a Peter Pan collar; it will lie flat on the bodice or shoulders and can be varied in width or have a decorative edge, eg, pointed scalloped, etc (fig 164a).

2 *Raised*: These are either set on a neckband or have an extra

depth built into the design which helps the collar to stand up slightly at the neck and roll back over itself into a straight or rever type collar (fig 164b).

Method for flat collars
1 Lay under to upper collar, RS together, matching balance marks.
2 Pin and tack on fitting line of outer edge of collar, from **A** to **B**. Do not tack inner neck edge (fig 165a).
3 Remove pins, machine on fitting line. Remove tacks, clip curves. Layer seams and press (fig 165a).
4 Turn collar through to RS, making sure seam joins are sharp (pull out seam with needle, but avoid damaging fabric). Tack and press round edge to hold flat whilst making up (fig 165b).

Method for straight or rever type collars
1 Place under collar to upper, RS together, matching balance marks, centre backs, etc.
2 Pin and tack outer edge from **A** to **B**. Do not tack neck edge (fig 166).
3 Remove pins and machine on fitting line from **A** to **B**, following tacking marks.
4 Remove tacks. Clip across outer angles and into any inner angles. Layer seams and press well (fig 166).
5 Turn through to RS. Make sure seam lies flat and crisp. Press well,

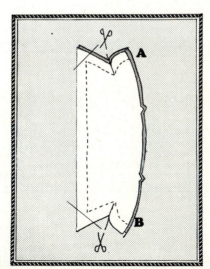

Figure 166

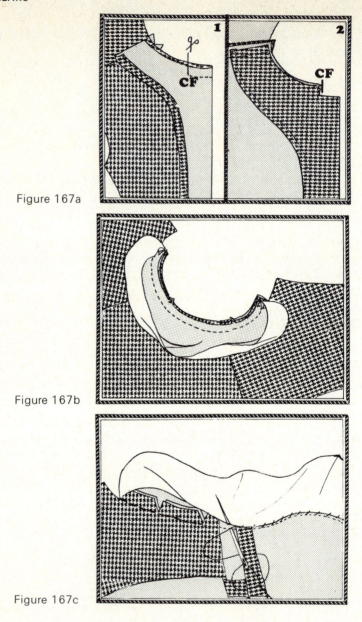

Figure 167a

Figure 167b

Figure 167c

tack outer edge to hold in position whilst working. (A neckband may have to be stitched in place at this point. Follow directions given on pattern as they vary in method of application.)

APPLYING COLLARS

When the collar is at the stage where it can be applied, there are two ways to put it on. One way uses a facing, and the other omits the facing.

Method for applying collars without a facing
1 Prepare garment bodice by making up. Turn back and complete front facings (fig 167a).
2 Matching all balance points and keeping upper collar clear, pin and tack under collar into place on RS of garment, easing and stretching where necessary (fig 167b).
3 Remove pins, machine on fitting line. Remove tacks, clip curves and layer seams. Press seam well *up into* collar.
4 Clip curves at neck edge of upper collar. Press under seam allowance of upper collar. Hem or slip stitch into place just on, or fractionally above, machine line (see chapter 7). Press thoroughly (fig 167c).
   For quickness, on clothes where finish is not too important, collar can be machined in place close to edge of fold.
5 Remove tacks on outer edge of collar.

Note: This method can only be used when neckline is always worn fastened (because hemming stitches would otherwise show across the open rever).

Method for applying collars with back neck facings
1 Make up collar. Turn through to RS. Tack neck edges together on fitting line.
2 Make up garment bodice sections and join back neck to front facings (RS together at shoulders). Press joins open (fig 168a).
3 Place collar on to garment, upper collar facing *up*, and under collar to RS of garment. Matching centre back and balance points, pin and tack on fitting lines at neck edge. Remove pins (fig 168b).
4 Place facing RS down on to collar, matching centre back etc. Pin and tack on fitting line at neck edge and centre front edges of bodice where necessary (fig 168c).
5 Remove pins and machine on fitting line. Remove tacks, clip curves, layer seams and press.
6 Turn facing on to WS of garment and neaten edges. Press (fig 168d).

Alternative method to using a facing
Repeat procedure as for a faced collar up to stage 4.
4 Cut length of 'bias' binding or crossway strip (see chapter 8) to

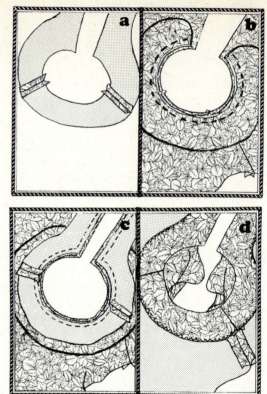

Figure 168

fit neck edge of collar. Attach collar as for a crossway facing (see chapter 19). Hem down to secure.

Collars can be machined close to fold on outer edge if wished and collars which stand up from the neck can be machined from **A** to **B**, following curve of neck edge (fig 169).

Golden rules for collars
1 Make sure collar pattern fits you before cutting out.
2 To prevent collar twisting, always cut on straight grain or true cross.
3 Match centre backs and balance points before easing and stretching rest of collar.
4 Clip curves and layer seams (see chapter 5) to allow collar to lie properly.

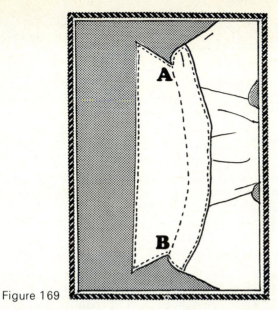

Figure 169

5 Cut across outer angles and clip inner angles of collars so they lie flat at these points (see chapter 5).
6 Use an interfacing of the right type and weight for your fabric (see chapter 9). This gives the work a professional finish.
7 Press well at each stage (see chapter 24).

Words and terms used in this chapter (see Glossary for meanings)
Sewing terms

balance marks	clip curves	layer seams
bias binding	cross(way)	seam allowance
clip angles	fitting line	

General terms

askew	detachable	fractionally
contrasting	distinctive	scalloped

Things to do
1 Design three new styles of collar and give methods for making up.
2 Collect magazine pictures of collar styles and stick them into a scrap book.
3 Where might you use a rever collar? List three different garments.

16. Cuffs

As there are two kinds of collar so there are two kinds of cuff:
1 Those which turn back on themselves or on to the sleeve.
2 Those which lie flat and fit the arm in a band.

Variations of style in the cuff usually follow the style of the collar, eg, a scalloped edged collar looks best with scalloped edged cuffs etc.

Cuffs can be an unbroken band (often suitable for elastic casing). They can be a split band set on to a sleeve without an opening (best for upperarm cuffs).

Or they can be set on to a sleeve with an opening, in which case they will have an overlap and a fastening of some kind (this type is best for wrist-fitting cuffs).

Method for a continuous band cuff
1 Gather or make up sleeve hem edge to fit required size.
2 Cut cuff band this length *plus* turnings × twice width of finished band *plus* 1·5 cm turnings, eg, upper arm circumference of 28 cm needing a 2·5 cm wide finished band will take a piece of fabric 31 cm × 8 cm (to fit closely).
3 Join arm band at short edges, RS together. Tack and machine on fitting line. Remove tacks and press seam open (fig 170a).
4 Crease band along half its length, ws inside. Press.
5 Place band on sleeve edge, RS and raw edges together. Match seam line of band to underarm sleeve seam where possible (fig 170b).

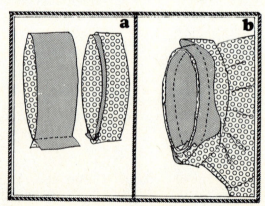

Figure 170

6 Pin and tack round circumference, through garment fabric and undersection of cuff only (two thicknesses).

7 Remove pins and machine on fitting line. Remove tacks, layer seams and press (fig 170b).

8 Fold under turning allowance on remaining raw edge of band and tack and hem to sleeve (chapter 7, Hand Stitches), slightly above machine line. Press raw edges of seam *up into band* before you work. Remove tacks. Press.

Method for setting on a cuff with a split band

1 Gather or make up sleeve hem edge to fit required size.

2 Cut band to fit, plus turnings. This can be a single piece of material folded in half lengthways, or two separate pieces joined together along one edge (the latter allows shaping of cuff if required).

3 Either: fold band in half and join down each short side (RS together), or: place the two sections of band together (RS and raw edges together) and seam along one long and two short sides (if making a shaped cuff). Trim or clip angles, layer seams, press. Turn through to RS. Press. Tack edges close to fold to stop them rolling.

4 Mark point of cuff opening on sleeve then, matching opening of cuff to this point, attach cuff so that one side faces RS of garment. The side next to garment can be upper *or* under section of cuff, depending on whether cuff is to be turned up or down. Pin and tack on fitting line through garment and undersection of cuff only (two thicknesses of fabric), keeping top section clear (fig 171a).

5 Remove pins and machine on fitting line. Remove tacks, layer seams and press. Snip seam layers to fitting line each side of split.

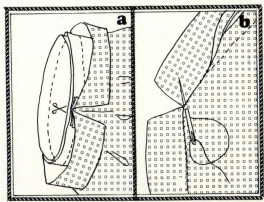

Figure 171

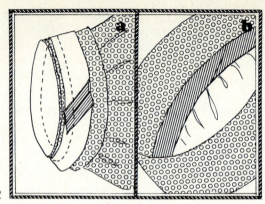

Figure 172

6 Press under a turning on remaining section of cuff and attach to seam line with hemming stitches (see chapter 7) (fig 171b).

Alternatively, both methods can have cuff attached with a narrow crossway facing or bias binding, as for collars:

1 Cuff is attached to sleeve with tacks around circumference, through all thicknesses (fig 172a).

2 A facing is placed on cuff, RS down and machined in place on fitting line through all thicknesses (fig 172b).

3 Remove tacks. Layer seams and press. A turning is pressed under on facing and hemmed or slip stitched to garment (fig 172b).

For more information on facings see chapter 19 and for crossway, see chapter 8.

Figure 173

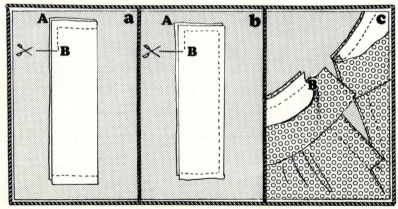

Method for cuffs attached to a sleeve with an opening
1 Complete sleeve (join seams and make up opening). Gather etc to fit cuff size.
2 Cut a cuff band to fit this size *plus* turnings, *plus* amount required for an overlap. A cuff band 5 cm × 18 cm will need either: a single piece of fabric 13 cm × 26 cm (1·5 cm turnings and 5 cm overlap), or: two pieces 8 cm × 26 cm.
3 Fold cuff along its length, RS in. Join at each end and from **A** to **B** at one end for overlap (fig 173a). Repeat with opposite end for other cuff. Alternatively: join two-pieces, RS together along one long and two short sides and **A** to **B** for overlap (fig 173b).
4 Clip angles, layer seams and press. Turn through to RS.
5 Attach cuff to sleeve, matching end with overlap point **B** to overlapping end of opening, as in Method 1 (fig 173c).

Openings in a sleeve which already has a large overlapping section, eg, a continuous wrap opening (see chapter 13) need not have the excess overlap in the cuff, but a good overlap on a cuff certainly makes it look better and the opening will be less likely to gape.

Golden rules for cuffs
1 Overlaps on cuffs are necessary for most types of opening but especially for bound or slit openings (see chapter 13).
2 Mark and make buttonholes on cuffs before applying to sleeve if possible as the smaller sections are easier to handle.
3 If making buttonloops set into a join, these should be placed in position on cuff before joining upper cuff to under section, and before attaching cuffs to sleeves.
4 Fit cuff pattern before cutting out so cuff fits snugly but not so tight it cuts off the blood supply!
5 An interfacing is essential for a good, crisp finish to cuffs (see chapter 9).
6 For button-link or cuff-link type fastenings, do allow at least 3 cm overlap on both sides of opening of cuff, making round ended, double buttonholes (see chapter 14) on each side to take links.
7 Complete cuffs and attach to sleeves before joining sleeves to bodice, where possible.
8 Note that one cuff is for *left* and one for *right*, arm; this is especially important on overlapping cuffs.
9 Cuffs can be top-stitched by machine or hand, 0·3 cm–0·5 cm from edge all round for a crisp neat finish (use straight stitch by machine or running stitch by hand).

Words and terms used in this chapter (see Glossary for meanings)
Sewing terms

bias binding	fitting line	scalloped
casing	interfacing	trim angles
clip angles	layer seams	turning allowance
crossway (facing)	overlap	under section

General terms

alternatively	continuous	previous
circumference	excess	variations

Things to do
1 Collect magazine pictures of cuffs and stick them in your scrap book.
2 List four different variations of cuff and where these might be used.
3 Make up a sleeve with a simple cuff, as a sample.

◎ ◎ ◎

17. Sleeves

The style or type of sleeve you choose on a garment will be influenced by the fabric you are using and the kind of life the garment is going to lead. For instance, some styles of sleeve such as magyar or kimono sleeves are ideal for fabrics that drape well or have large patterns difficult to match up with a seamed style.

Evening dresses look great with long flowing sleeves; shorter, easy-fitting sleeves are better for activities such as shopping, working or sport.

There are so many sleeve styles and variations, the range can be overwhelming, but most of the variations fall into one of the following types of armhole setting: round set-in, raglan, magyar or kimono, and dropped sleeve line.

SET-IN SLEEVES
Definition: The sleeve is set into an armhole which follows the top of the shoulder in a curved line to under the arm (fig 174).

This type of sleeve setting can be made puffed, tucked, gathered,

Figure 174

darted, plain or whatever; the method for setting-in for all kinds follows a basic procedure.

Method for setting sleeves into a round or rounded armhole

1 Make up garment bodice sections, eg, join at shoulder and underarm.

2 Press seams open if they are flat seams (see chapter 12). Turn sleeve through to RS.

3 Gather sleeve between points **A** and **B** so it fits armhole (see chapter 11 for gathering and easing) (fig 175a). Join underarm seam and turn sleeve through to right side.

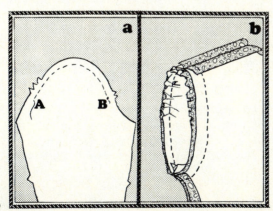

Figure 175

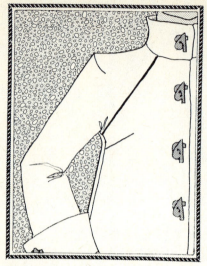
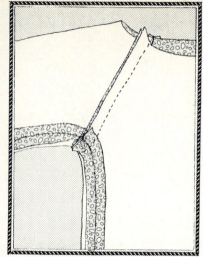

Figure 176   Figure 177

4 Keeping sleeve underarm seam matched with bodice underarm seam and right side and raw edges together, match centre point of top of sleeve head to centre point of shoulder on bodice. Pin in place. Pin at all balance points.

5 It may be necessary at this stage to tighten up or ease off gathering threads of sleeve head until they match armhole. A perfectly set-in plain sleeve will not have any puckers showing on right side, but a nice smooth curve to the top of sleeve.

6 When you are satisfied that the sleeve is pinned correctly, tack in place on fitting line using a backstitch every 2–3 cm to hold firmly (fig 175b). Remove pins. Turn through to RS to check that sleeve is *setting* properly. Try on garment to make sure.

7 If sleeve looks right, machine on fitting line, remove gathering stitches and tacks and neaten raw edges. Seam turnings are usually both pressed towards sleeve, extra bulk of material giving sleeve head a slight 'lift' which makes it look better.

RAGLAN SLEEVE

Definition: Set into a diagonally slanted armhole, the line of the sleeve following the line of the armhole to the neck. These sleeves do not have shoulder joins as the armhole seams go as far as the neck (fig 176).

Sometimes raglan sleeves have a dart which gives extra shape.

They are suitable for bulky fabrics on outer garments where extra room is required and on knits and woollens of all kinds.

Method
1 Join underarm seams of garment. Press.
2 Join underarm seams of sleeves. Press. (Make up sleeve darts where necessary at this stage.) Turn through to RS.
3 Place underarm seam of bodice to underarm seam of sleeve RS together. Pin.
4 Matching balance points and top sections, pin and tack each armhole sections.
5 Remove pins, machine on fitting line (fig 177). Remove tacks and press. Finish by applying collar etc.

MAGYAR SLEEVES
Definition: These sleeves are usually cut in one with the bodice. As a rule they have no armhole seams, but can have a seam going from shoulder down to the wrist (fig 178) or only one seam under the arm to the wrist.

No method need be given for setting-in these sleeves as there is no setting-in to do. However, because they are subjected to a lot of strain under the arm they need strengthening at this point. This type of sleeve, like the raglan sleeve, is easy to make.

Figure 178

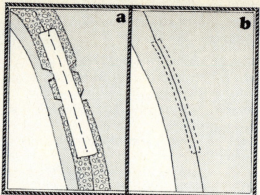

Figure 179

Method: Taping the seam
1 Make up underarm seam and press open.
2 Cut a length of tape to fit the part to take strain, about 8–10 cm of 1·5–2·5 cm tape is suitable for most purposes.
3 Tack in position over seam on ws of garment (fig 179a).
4 On RS, machine 0·3 cm from seam line each side and across top and bottom of tape using straight stitch, or, machine one or two rows of zig-zag using a swing needle machine. Tacking line should show where tape begins and ends. Remove tacks and press (fig 179b).

This method of strengthening is good for any seams which are

Figure 180

likely to take a lot of strain, eg, the inner leg seam of trousers at the crotch. An alternative method of strengthening is to tape the seams (tack tape over fitting line) before joining seams together.

DROPPED AND KIMONO SLEEVES
Definition: Sleeve is set into an armhole which is not shaped but squared off, often to a few cm below shoulderline.

These sleeves were originally used on fishermen's smocks and traditional Japanese kimonos, but have been adopted as a design feature. Because there is no shaping, gathering or easing, they are extremely easy to make (fig 180). Kimono sleeves are large square sleeves set into a dropped shoulder line.

Method
1 Join shoulder and underarm seams of garment. Press open.
2 Join underarm seam of sleeve. Press open and turn through to RS.
3 Matching underarm and centre top sleeve, pin and tack sleeve to garment (fig 181).
4 Remove pins and machine on fitting line. Remove tacks and press seam to sleeve side.

Alternative (Flat) method for setting-in sleeves
The previous four methods all state that the underarm seam of the

Figure 181

Figure 182

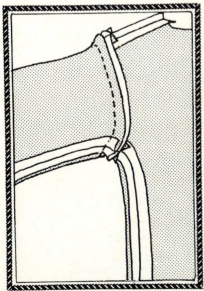
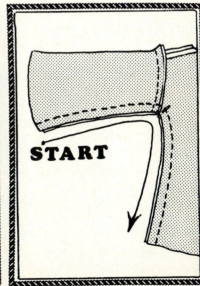

garment and sleeve are made before setting-in the sleeves. However, some people find it much easier to set-in a sleeve by a *flat method*. This means underarm and sleeve seams are joined last, so the garment can be flat while sleeves are being applied. Where possible I would suggest that you use a flat method – especially if you are a beginner.

The only sleeve for which you cannot use this method is the kind with two underarm seams, sometimes found on coats with panels.

Cuffs and sleeve edges cannot be finished until later, when you use a flat method.

Method for set-in sleeves
Repeat as for ordinary method but do not join underarm seams of garment or sleeve until final stage. Then, matching armhole seams and balance points, join pieces from cuff edge to bodice hem in one go (fig 182).

Method for dropped sleeves
Join the shoulder seams of garment and armhole seams before joining underarm seams.

Golden rules for sleeves

1 Make sure sleeve is cut on straight grain or true cross (eg, bias cut sleeves), otherwise it will twist to one side. (For cutting out, see chapter 5.)
2 Always make a right and a left sleeve because front and back armholes are a different shape.
3 Except for flat methods of making up, join cuffs etc before setting in sleeve.
4 Use a pin to ease threads of sleeve head closer together.
5 Make darts, tucks, gathers, etc, at sleeve head before setting-in sleeve.
6 Some patterns have dropped front shoulder seams, so the centre point of shoulder may be slightly higher than shoulder seam in this case.
7 Always check, by measuring round fitting lines of pattern, that armhole is correct size for wearer. An armhole which is too tight can cause soreness, apart from looking terrible.

Words and terms used in this chapter (see Glossary for meanings)
Sewing terms

balance points	drape	easing
dart	dropped sleeveline	fitting line

gather(ed)
kimono sleeve
magyar sleeve
puff(ed) sleeve

raglan sleeve

set-in sleeve
straight grain

true cross
tuck(ed)

General terms
bulk
diagonally

identical
influenced

procedure
variations

Things to do

1 Draw six different sleeve designs, giving their names.
2 Collect pictures of favourite sleeve styles, giving reasons for choice.
3 Are some sleeve styles more suitable than others for certain fabrics? If you think so, give reasons why.

PART FIVE

Neatening Edges

There are many kinds of edge finishes and there are many kinds of edges to be neatened. Which one you choose will depend on the type of edge that needs to be finished.

Edges which should be neatened on garments are as follows:

1 Seam turnings
2 Hems
3 Armholes
4 Wrist edges

5 Necklines
6 Waists (of skirts and trousers)
7 Openings of all types.

The usual finishes to neaten all kinds of edges are as follows: binding, piping, facings, hems, plus a variety of hand and machine stitched edges for neatening seams etc.

The choice of an edge finishing will be influenced by two things: 1 the kind of edge to be neatened, and 2 the style and fabric of the garment or article.

A collarless wool jacket, for instance, looks and wears better with a neck facing whilst a nightie or blouse may only need a bound edge. Some styles of garments look better with a particular edge finish. For example, an intricately shaped bodice top will be easier to finish with a shaped facing than with a hem or binding.

The chapters following give information and methods of construction for most types of edge finish.

18. Seam Finishes

It is usually necessary to finish the raw edges of the seam allowance inside the garment for two reasons:
1 For a neat appearance on the ws.
2 Seams which are finished off are stronger and therefore able to take more wear.

Seams can be finished off by one of three major ways: machine-sewn edges, bound edges and, for quickness, pinked edges.

PINKING
The edges of the seam allowance are trimmed evenly with pinking

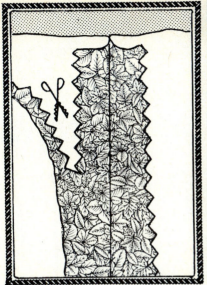 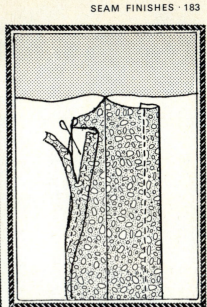

Figure 183   Figure 184

shears, which have a serrated or zig-zag edge to the blades. Pinking is only suitable for articles which will not be laundered often (such as seams in upholstery) or for fabrics which are unlikely to fray much, eg, felt or closely woven fabrics (fig 183).

MACHINED EDGE
Straight stitch: Trim seam allowance evenly, set machine stitch to width 0, length 2, turn under a narrow turning and machine close to fold. Trim surplus to 0·3 cm from stitching line (fig 184).

Swing needle: A zig-zag stitch can be used to neaten seams. There are three methods which can be used:

Method 1
Set machine to a suitable stitch length and width (test on spare fabric first). Machine about 1·5 cm from fitting line of seam using edge of presser foot as a guide (see chapter 6). Trim surplus close to stitching, being sure not to cut on to it (fig 185).

Method 2
Same as method 1 but first make a narrow turning on seam allowance evenly along its length. Zig-zag machine along this fold (fig 186). This method is only suitable for very fine fabrics.

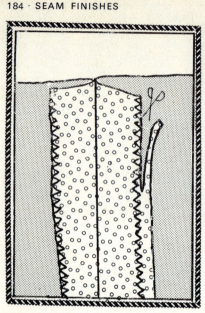

Figure 185   Figure 186

Method 3
This method both neatens and makes a quick French seam in one operation. After making an open seam, 1 Zig-zag together both sides of seam allowance. 2 Trim to stitching. 3 Press flat to one side (fig 139, chapter 12, Seams).

BOUND SEAM EDGES
Bias or crossway bindings which stretch slightly are used for all seams going around the body, eg, armhole and waist. Straight or Paris seam bindings, which do not stretch, are used for seams going up and down the body. (For instructions for bound seams see chapter 20, Bindings, Method A.)

HAND-SEWN EDGES
Use blanket stitch or overcasting (see chapter 7, Hand Stitches). This is a long, slow method which is rarely used today.

Words and terms used in this chapter (see Glossary for meanings)
Sewing terms

bias	fitting line	seam allowance
close weave	non-fray	zig-zag
cross(way)	Paris binding	

General terms
surplus

Things to do
Make up samples of various seam neatening methods. Write notes
about stitches used and where you might use these methods.

◎   ◎   ◎

19. Facings

Definition: A facing is a piece of fabric used to neaten an edge on a
garment, cut to the same shape as that edge and seamed together
with it.

Facings can be made on to the right or wrong side of a garment.
If made on to the RS they are known as *conspicuous facings*, and are
usually decorative; if made on to the WS they are known as *inconspicuous facings* and are fairly unnoticeable from the RS.
   There are three main types of facings:

Straight facings: Facing strip is cut on straight grain for straight
edges, eg, shirt fronts.
Crossway facings: Used for narrow curved facings, eg, faced hem
edges of skirts.
Shaped facings: Facing is cut to same shape as garment edge and can
be of any depth. Usually found at armhole and neck front edges of
garments (also faced slit openings, see chapter 13).

Straight facings
These have a limited use as they can only be made on to straight
edges such as are found on button-through skirts (fig 187), or the
straight hems of some types of skirt. They are also occasionally used
on faced hems (false hems) of household articles.

Method for straight facings
1 Measure length of edge to be faced, making sure it is straight
(use wooden rule as a guide).
2 Decide on width of finished facing, then cut a piece of fabric on
straight grain (see chapter 5) the length of edge to be faced, *plus*

Figure 187   Figure 188

turnings. The width should be: width of finished facing, *plus* 1·5 cm turnings, eg, a finished facing 28 cm × 4 cm will need a strip of fabric approximately 31 cm × 7 cm.

3 Place facing strip on to garment edge (RS together for *inconspicuous* facing). Pin and tack on fitting line (fig 188).

4 Remove pins. Machine on fitting line, remove tacks.

5 Press back, keeping seam edge sharp by rolling it between thumb and forefinger and tacking flat before pressing. It helps to pull out seam with a pin, but be sure not to damage fabric.

6 Finish raw edges of facing with a neatening method given for seams (see chapter 18, Seam Finishes) and catch or slip stitch into place where necessary.

If facing is to be made on to RS of garment, same process will be used, but RS of facing will be placed to WS of garment (fig 144, chapter 13, Openings).

A facing made on to the RS should have a narrow turning made on one edge, tacked and machined into place approximately 0·3–0·5 cm from fold, depending on width of facing.

Shaped facings

These are cut to the exact shape of the edge to be faced and will be deep enough to give a neat, flat finish (fig 189). Some shaped

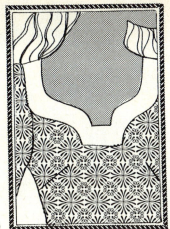

Figure 189

facings are cut 'all-in-one', eg, armhole and neck facings on sleeve-less dresses.

Method for neck facings, collarless
1 Join shoulder seams of garment together. Join shoulder seams of neck facing. Press open.
2 Mark fitting lines of neck edge on both facings and garment.
3 Matching balance points and shoulder seams, position facing on to garment (RS together for inconspicuous facings). Pin and tack into place on fitting line.

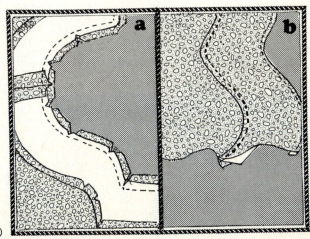

Figure 190

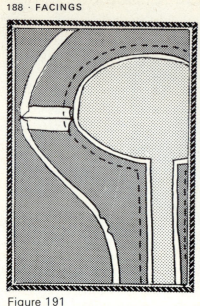

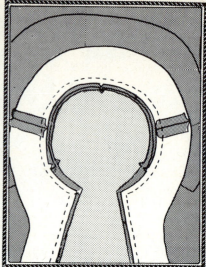

Figure 191   Figure 192

4 Remove pins, machine on fitting line. Clip curves almost to stitching (fig 190a).
5 Layer raw edges of facing join, to avoid bulkiness.
6 Press back facing so it is flat and machine 0·3 cm from fitting line through three thicknesses of fabric (fig 190b). This will prevent fabric rolling up.
7 Finish raw edges of facing with a neatening method as given for seams (see chapter 18, Seam Finishes). Press facing flat on to garment from wrong side.

ALL-IN-ONE NECK FACING
Same process as for plain neck facing except that front facing is included at this stage of making up of garment (fig 191). Trim angles at neck edge for sharpness to the angles (see chapter 6). Also if material has a noticeable right and a wrong side, be sure to get right and left facings joined to back neck facing correctly.

Facings with collars
After tacking collar into place (see chapter 15, Collars) position facing on to garment, RS and raw edges together, matching balance points, shoulder seams, etc. Tack and machine on fitting line through all thicknesses. Repeat stages **4–7** of collarless neck facing method as in figs 190a and b (fig 192).

Armhole facings

Same process as for collarless neck facings except that both underarm and shoulder seams are joined before putting facing on, and
joins are usually made in underarm part of facing (fig 193a).

Where the arm and neck facings are not cut together, the armhole
facings should be made first, then the neck facing, so that the latter
will lie flat over the armhole facing. A few catch stitches (see chapter
7, Hand Stitches) will secure the two together where they overlap
(fig 193b).

All-in-one armhole and neck facing method (for lining bodices)

1 Mark fitting lines on garment and facing. Be sure that each piece
(at shoulder) measures same between fitting lines.
2 Join side seams of garment and side seams of facing. Press seams
open.
3 Place facing on to garment, RS together, matching centre fronts,
balance points and side seams.
4 Pin and tack on fitting lines all round neck edge and armhole,
omitting four shoulder seams (fig 194a).
5 Remove pins, machine on fitting lines. Clip curves, remove tacks.
Press.
6 Turn facing through to WS. Press well from back so join is neat
and crisp.
7 Turn garment inside out, pin and tack shoulder seams together
through two garment thicknesses, making sure they match
perfectly (fig 194b).
8 Remove pins, machine on fitting line. Remove tacks. Press seam
open.

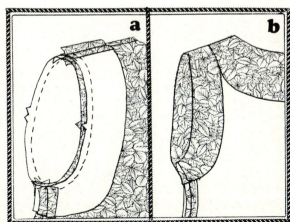

Figure 193

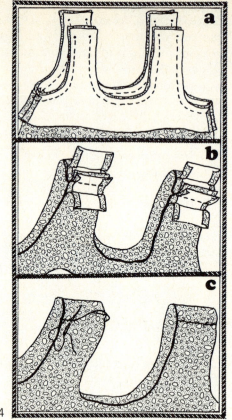

Figure 194

9 Overlap one shoulder facing section on to the other, enclosing raw edges. Slip stitch into place (fig 194c). Press well from ws.

Crossway facings

These are usually fairly narrow facings (up to 2·5 cm wide) made of strips of joined crossway and used on gently curving edges such as neck, armholes and curved hems, where a little 'give' is required. They can also be used on straight edges for a decorative effect if made on to the RS of the garment.

Method for crossway facings
1 Join seams of garment edge to be faced and mark fitting lines. Trim edges parallel to fitting lines.
2 Measure length or circumference of edge to be faced. Cut and join crossway strips (see chapter 8) to fit, *plus* turnings. The width

of the facing strip will be the finished width *plus* turnings, eg, for a 2·5 cm facing cut strips approximately 4 cm wide (depending on frayability of fabric).

3 If edge is circular, eg, armhole, join facing strip before placing on garment. If not, eg, neckline with back opening, place strip on as it is. Place RS of facing to RS of garment (for *inconspicuous facing*), or to WS of garment (for *conspicuous facing*). Keeping raw edges together, pin and tack on fitting line easing and stretching where necessary (figs 94a and b, chapter 8, Crossway).

4 Remove pins and machine on fitting line. Remove tacks, clip curves, layer raw edges. Press well.

5 If facing is made on to WS, finish raw edges with one of neatening methods given in chapter 18 for seams, and catch stitch into place at shoulders etc. If facing is made on to RS, press under narrow turning, tack into place on garment. Machine close to fold, remove tacks and press (fig 144, chapter 13, Openings).

An interesting decorative effect can be made with crossway facings using striped or checked materials, especially on square necks, pockets, or necks and armholes with angles (fig 195). It takes a little extra care in cutting and joining but gives a really original look to a garment.

For faced hems to skirts see chapter 23, Hems.

Figure 195

Golden rules for facings

1 Where possible cut facings from same fabric as garment (or finer if garment fabric is very thick).

2 Decide whether facing is to show on RS, or to be made on to WS of garment. In the latter case it will not show. If it is to show and the fabric is patterned, remember to take this into account when planning the facing.

3 If material has a noticeable RS and WS or if it has a nap or pile (see chapter 3) these factors should all be taken into account when cutting out the facing especially for conspicuous facings.

4 Most neck and armhole facings are applied after garment is made up and after openings have been completed.

5 Make facings wide enough to lie flat on garment, especially if not being stitched down.

6 Neaten raw edges of facing on inside by one of methods given in chapter 18.

7 Cut facings on straight grain or true cross (see chapters 5 and 8).

Words and terms used in this chapter (see Glossary for meanings)

Sewing terms

balance points	false hems	straight grain
clip angles	fitting line	trim angles
crossway	fray(ability)	

General terms

circumference	manipulate	overlap
conspicuous	omitting	parallel
inconspicuous		

Things to do

1 State where you might use a conspicuous facing.

2 Explain what a crossway facing is and where you might use it.

3 Supposing you had a cotton skirt which was too short, explain how you might change it so that it was still wearable.

20. Bindings

Definition: A process by which a strip of fabric encloses the raw edges of a garment, and its own raw edges, giving a neat finish which can be seen from both sides of the garment.

This method can be used for neatening seam edges and neck, armhole and sleeve edges of garments (for bound openings see chapter 13). It is not as strong as a hem or a facing, but can look very decorative. It is *conspicuous* because the binding strip can be seen from the right and the wrong side of the fabric. Because there are usually *five* layers of fabric to a binding it is only suitable for medium to fine fabrics (straight bindings as mentioned below will only have *three* layers and are suitable for thicker fabrics and seam neatening).

There are two kinds of binding:

Crossway: This is cut on the true cross (see chapter 8) and is known commercially as 'bias binding'.
Straight: Ribbon, braid, Paris binding, seam bindings, are used on any straight edge, eg, seams.

It is usual to have crossway binding on edges which go around the body, eg, armhole or waist, and straight binding for edges of seams which go up and down, eg, side front and back seams. A crossway binding will allow 'give', whereas straight binding will not stretch at all.

Binding method A

1 Cut strip of crossway fabric 2·5 cm longer (take into account diagonal-shaped ends!) than edge to be bound × required width (see cutting and joining crossway, chapter 8). For 0·5 cm finished binding cut crossway 2·5 cm wide. Commercial bindings usually give a finished bind of 0·5–1 cm and are suitable for most edges to be neatened in this way.
2 Trim edge to be neatened evenly from fitting line, eg, for 0·5 cm finished binding on armhole edge, trim edge to 0·5 cm from fitting line (not necessary for bound seam edges). Clip curves to stay stitching (see chapter 6) (fig 196a).
3 Press binding strip in half lengthways to give a guide to fold, then open out again. Lay RS of binding to RS of garment, raw edges together.

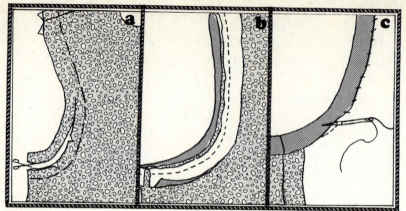

Figure 196

4 Pin and tack on fitting line, easing curves where necessary (for angles see below).

5 Remove pins. Machine on fitting line (fig 196b).

6 Remove tacks. Press binding over raw edge of garment. Press under narrow turning on binding. Folded edge of binding should lie flat over raw edge of garment. (If it doesn't, not enough surplus has been trimmed away from garment.)

7 Tack down binding on ws of garment slightly above machine line.

8 Slip stitch or hem into position just above machine stitching, so stitches do not show from RS (see chapter 7, Hand Stitches) (fig 196c).

If the edge is continuous (eg, armhole or sleeve edge) cut binding to finished length *plus* turnings and join strip diagonally before placing on edge of garment to be neatened (fig 95, chapter 8, Crossway).

For a professional look, binding, like piping, should be of even depth along its length. If a little care is taken in the construction, this should be easy.

There are special sewing machine attachments which will automatically bind edges, but as these are sometimes difficult to use and mistakes hard to alter, it is not advisable to use them unless you are able to control a sewing machine really well. If you have lots of edges to bind, there is an alternative method which is quicker than the first one given as it does not entail hemming. The finished effect of this method has one line of machining which shows on both sides of the garment.

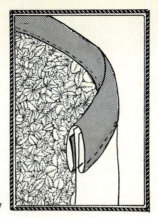

Figure 197

Binding method B: Quick method

Complete as for method **A** to the end of stage **2**.

3 Press binding strip in half lengthways and press under two narrow turnings on each raw edge (WS inside).

4 Place binding so centre fold matches up with raw edge of garment. Pin and tack through all thicknesses close to inner edge (fig 197).

5 Remove pins. Machine on tacking line (approximately 0·2 cm from inner edge).

6 Remove tacks, press binding on WS.

For this type of binding it is essential to make sure that *all thicknesses* of fabric are stitched through.

Paris or seam binding can be put on by this method (omit stages 1–3) as there are no raw edges to turn in.

Binding angles and corners

Outer corners

Allow a fold to form at corner. Keep fold out of way whilst machining binding down. Hand stitch fold flat (fig 198a). Turn binding to WS. Hem or slip stitch in usual way (fig 198b).

Inner corners

Pin and tack binding into position following line of angle. Lower part of binding will curl up (fig 198a). Turn binding to WS. Hem or slip stitch in usual way (fig 198b).

For bound seam edges attach binding as you would for binding a straight hem, omitting the join.

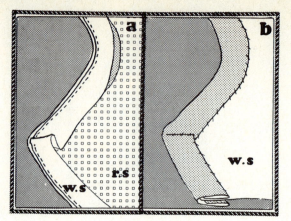

Figure 198

For bound buttonholes see chapter 14, Fastenings.
For bound hems see chapter 23, Hems.
For bound pockets see chapter 24, Pockets.
For Golden rules and list of words used see end of chapter 21, Pipings.

Things to do
1 Make up a sample crossway binding on a curved edge.
2 Make up a sample straight grain binding on an angled edge.
3 List four places where you could use binding.

◎ ◎ ◎

21. Pipings

Definition: A piping is a piece of fabric folded in half lengthways and inserted into the join of two other pieces of fabric.

Pipings can be inserted into a seam or a faced edge to give emphasis to a style line or for a decorative effect. They can be padded with cording but will be stiffer than if left unpadded and therefore less suitable for certain purposes. Pipings can be cut on the cross or the straight grain. For piping a faced edge, eg, armhole, neckline, sleeve or hem, the construction will be as follows:

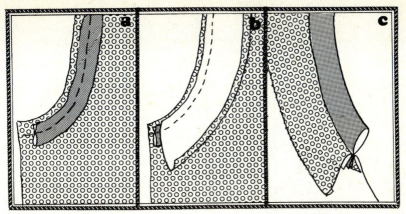

Figure 199

Method for piped edges

1 Mark fitting lines on garment edge and facing piece with a line of tacks.

2 Trim edges of garment evenly to seam allowance; this will vary but should be *less* than finished width of edge facing (for facings, see chapter 19), eg, for finished facing width 2 cm, trim seam allowance to 1 cm.

3 Measure circumference or length of edge to be piped. Cut length of piping fabric slightly longer than measured length (to allow for joining if necessary) × twice width of finished piping *plus* seam allowances, eg, 0·5 cm piping for 28 cm armhole edge, cut fabric 31 cm × 4 cm (1·5 cm turnings). For cutting crossway strips, see chapter 8.

4 Join piping strip edges RS together (if applicable).

5 Fold strip in half lengthways (WS together). Tack through both thicknesses 0·5 cm from fold (for 0·5 cm finished piping).

6 Place piping on RS of edge of garment, matching fitting lines of garment to tacking lines of piping. Keep all raw edges together (fig 199a).

7 Place facing RS down over piping, matching fitting lines etc. Pin and tack through all thicknesses (fig 199b).

8 Check piping looks even from RS of work. Remove pins, machine on fitting line. Remove tacks, clip curves.

9 Press on WS, open out and press facing to WS of garment. Finish raw edges of facing (see chapter 18, Seam Finishes) (fig 199c).

Method for corded piped edges

Same process as for piped eges with one difference: piping cord is

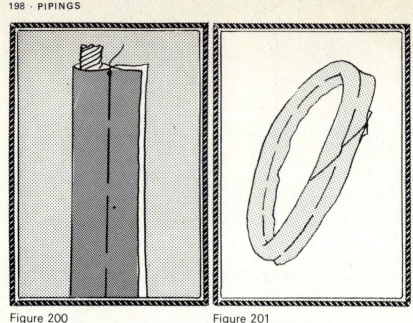

Figure 200   Figure 201

inserted into fold of piping strip and tacking made close to cording along its length (fig 200).

It is often easier to position a corded piping into a seam as the fitting line will be just below the bump of the cord and it is easy to feel this through the fabric, especially with a piping foot or zipper foot on the machine.

For joins in piping

Measure exact length of edge to be piped and add 5 cm. Cut a length of crossway fabric to this measurement (allowing for diagonal-shaped ends). Join this length on cross (see chapter 8) as in fig 201. Careful measuring is needed to ensure strip will fit circumference of edge to be piped, exactly. For a corded piping, cut the exact length of the edge to be piped from cord, plus a few cm; unravel excess at each end, and intertwine one on to other to form a smooth join. Place cord into fold of strip and tack into place (as for ordinary piping).

Angles in piping

Outer corners: Make pleat on seam allowance on an outer corner (fig 202).
Inner corners: Snip turning at inner corners (fig 202).

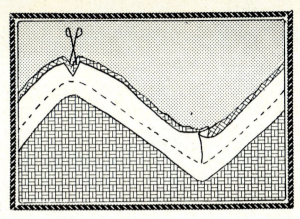

Figure 202

For more information on pipings see chapter 12, under Piped seams.

Golden rules for bindings and pipings
1 Be sure that binding or piping is of an even width along its length. Unevenness gives a badly made look.
2 Tack into position first before machining: this saves time and trouble later.
3 Choose correct *size* binding or piping width for *garment*, eg, the smaller the garment the narrower the binding or piping.
4 Choose correct *size* binding or piping width for *fabric* used, eg, a woollen cloak needs a wide binding to cover all raw edges.
5 Choose correct *fabric* binding or piping for *fabric* to be edged or decorated, eg, fine cotton fabrics need fine cotton pipings or bindings, woollen fabrics may look best with woollen bindings. Correct choice is most important for washing purposes etc.
6 When cutting binding or piping, remember that all curved edges or seams going round the body, will need piping or binding with some 'give' in it. Therefore they must be cut on true cross (see chapter 8). For straight edges or seams, cut on straight grain (see chapter 5).

Words and terms used in these chapters (see Glossary for meanings)
Sewing terms

clip curves	fitting line	stay stitching
cord(ing)	seam allowance	straight grain
cross(way)		

General terms

circumference	continuous	excess
commercial(ly)	diagonally	intertwine
conspicuous	emphasis	surplus
construction	entail	unravel

Things to do
1 Make up a crossway piping on to a circular edge.
2 Make up a corded piping.
3 Collect pictures of garments where piping is used as a design feature.

◎   ◎   ◎

22. Waist Finishes

Most skirts and trousers need to be finished at the waist. This is to hide raw edges and to prevent the waistline stretching during wear. There are three main ways of doing this:
1 Set the waistline into a band.
2 Face the waistline with petersham ribbon or facing.
3 Attach the skirt or trouser sections to some kind of bodice top by means of seaming.

There are other ways such as making a hem at waist and using this as a casing for elastic but these are not used quite so often.

Waistbands
These can be of any depth but must fit snugly without being too tight. Waistbands can have belt carriers for threading leather, plastic or fabric belts through. (Belts are sometimes necessary on trousers or jeans to stop them slipping down.) Some waistbands are curved or shaped in places.

Method for making a simple waistband
1 Make darts, pleats, etc, in waistline of garment so that it fits the waist with 3 cm ease for comfort. (Finish off openings.)
2 Cut length of fabric along straight grain to fit waist measurement, *plus* 2·5 cm for overlap (*plus* 1·5 cm turnings) × twice width

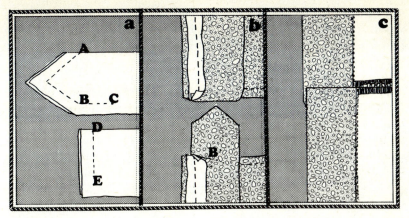

Figure 203

(*plus* 1·5 cm turnings). Eg, a 66 cm waistband, 5 cm wide needs fabric 71·5 cm long × 13 cm wide (1·5 cm turnings). Interface waistband at this stage, or stiffen it with belt backing remembering only half width of band (less seam allowance) need be interfaced.

3 Fold waistband in half along length RS in. Cut shaped section at one end if wished. Tack and machine from point A to B, and from B to C (B to C = length of overlap). Tack and machine D to E at other end (fig 203a).

4 Remove tacks. Clip angles. Layer seams. Press and turn through to RS.

5 Fold in half lengthways and press along fold.

6 Place waistband on garment, RS together, matching balance points, straight end of band to underlapping edge of opening on skirt, and shaped end of band (point B) to the other side (fig 203b).

7 Tack and machine in place through both thicknesses (garment and under part of waistband).

8 Remove tacks. Layer seams and press seam up into waistband.

9 Fold under 1·5 cm turning on remaining raw edge. Tack in place and hem to waist of garment slightly above first line of machining, enclosing all raw edges (fig 203c). Press well on WS.

Facing waistline with petersham ribbon
This method is ideal for a soft, natural look to the waistline as opposed to a tailored one.

Method   .
1 Adjust fullness in garment waistline by means of darts, pleats,

etc, to fit required waist size plus 3 cm ease. Finish openings.

2 Cut length of petersham ribbon to fit your waist, plus turnings (at end). (For a facing wider than 2·5 cm, buy curved type petersham which is especially made for facing waists.)

3 Apply petersham to waistline ws of petersham to RS of garment (just below fitting line) on seam allowance. The ribbon will not need to have any turnings as it has already been neatened. Tack and machine in place on fitting line (keep ribbon edges as close to fitting line as possible). Turn in two raw edges at each end and machine flat to garment, avoiding zips or fastenings (fig 204a).

4 Remove tacks. Trim seam of garment (but not ribbon). Turn to ws of skirt. Press well. Wide facings which are not shaped can be clipped and neatened (fig 204b).

Ordinary self facing can be applied to waists of trousers or skirts provided an interfacing is used or waist seam reinforced with tape to prevent stretching. Apply facing as for neck or hem facing (see chapters 19 and 23).

Attaching skirts etc to bodices

This can be done by means of an overlaid seam. Open or plain seam can be used but all layers should be pressed in the same direction. (See chapter 12, Seams.)

Method

1 Make up seams of both sections.

2 Adjust fullness in skirt or trouser waistline to required size. Prepare opening.

3 Matching centre back, front, sides, openings and all balance

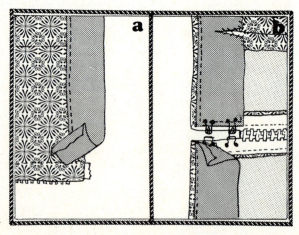

Figure 204

points of top and bottom sections, overlay top sections on to bottom, using an overlaying seam. Or place RS together at waistline and make an open seam.

If fullness is required in the gathers of a skirt, press the seam turnings down (this gives a puffed effect), otherwise press them upwards to cause less strain on bodice sections.

Golden rules for waistbands

1 Fit waistband pattern before cutting out. Never make a waistband too loose or too tight.

2 Do not make a waistband so wide it cuts into the ribs. Very wide bands need to be shaped to the body.

3 Allow enough overlap on a waistband for fastenings.

4 Choose strong fastenings for waistbands as they must take a lot of strain.

5 Apply a waistband or waistline finish to garment after making up but before finishing hem.

6 Cut waistband on straight grain to avoid stretching.

Words and terms used in this chapter (see Glossary for meanings)

Sewing terms

balance points	fray	overlaid seam
bodice	interface(d)(ing)	overlap
clip angles	layer seams	petersham
fitting line	open seams	tailor(ed)

General terms

| adequate | reinforced |

Things to do

Collect pictures of waist finishes, especially the more unusual ones. Work out possible methods for making them up.

23. Hems

Definition: A double fold of material normally on to the wrong side of the work with the first turning usually narrower than the second, secured with hand or machine stitching. *Also*: A single fold of material on to one side of the work, with the raw edges finished and secured to the garment or article.

Hems are used to finish the edges of garments, especially at the lower edge or those going around the body, eg, wrists; and also those edges on household articles which need a strong finish so that they will take a lot of wear.

The success of a hem depends as much on the preparation as on the actual sewing of it. The secureness of a hem will depend on how well it is sewn up; if you skimp on stitching time, the chances are the hem will come down (this often happens on badly made, shop-bought clothes).

Preparation

1 Get wearer to try on garment. Fasten all openings, put belts etc into place. Stand wearer on small table or chair so whoever is fitting garment can see straight away, the hang of the hem.
2 Decide on length of hem. If hem is not level, fitter should measure up from table or floor to the garment, evenly all the way around the hem, inserting pins at those points. Excess material is trimmed parallel to this line.
3 It is best if wearer has on the shoes or boots she would normally wear with the garment as this can make a difference to hang of hem.
4 Remove garment. Check that line of pins is even, then fold hem up at this line. Tack through both thicknesses about 1·5 cm from fold (fig 205).
5 Using tape measure or hem gauge (see chapter 4) measure off required hem depth (plus turnings) from folded edge and mark with pins or tailor's chalk. Trim excess fabric to this level (fig 206).

The hem and turning allowance for the hem will depend on two things: **a** where hem is placed on garment and **b** the fabric used. A sleeve hem on a jacket, for instance, is usually narrower than the hem of a skirt. Skirts need larger hems to help them hang properly. Some fine fabrics such as voile, look better with very narrow hems and thicker fabrics look better with wider hems.

For straight-edge hems, prepare hem by pulling a thread along

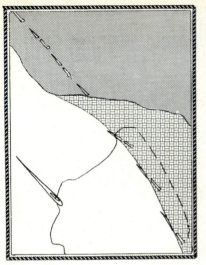 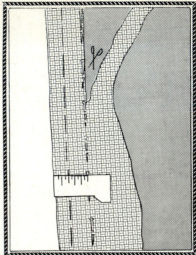

Figure 205   Figure 206

hem edge and trim to this. This will give a perfectly straight edge (for other methods of straightening, see chapter 5).

CURVED OR FLARED HEMS
These will need special preparation. When hem depth has been calculated and hem turning folded, you will notice that there is too much material at raw edge of hem. This can be dealt with in a number of ways, but some methods are more suitable for certain fabrics than others.

Method **A**: *Shrinking the fabric*
Suitable for wool and some cottons and linens etc (those which have not been pre-shrunk):
1 Mark position of hem edge and fold up to this line.
2 Trim hem turning to required depth.
3 Gather evenly all around hem, close to raw edge, using small running stitches (see chapter 7) or a machine gathering stitch (set to largest straight stitch) and adjust gathers until hem lies perfectly flat on garment.
4 Place dry cloth between garment and hem, then a damp cloth over hem, and press thoroughly. If pressing is done properly (see chapter 24), fabric will shrink to correct shape (fig 207).
5 Remove cloths and allow garment to dry. Remove tacks. Finish hem by one of methods given for hem finishes (see overleaf).

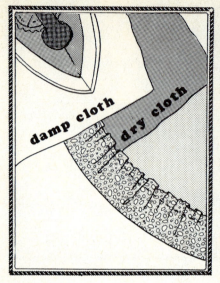

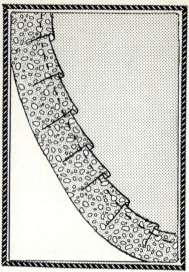

Figure 207   Figure 208

Method **B**: *Gathering*
Suitable for most non-shrinkable materials. Repeat method **A** to
stage **3**, then finish raw edge and secure hem by one of methods
given (see below). A flat binding is an easily applied finish to this
type of hem – use method **c** binding, page 209.

Method **C**: *Pleats or tucks*
Small pleats can be made all round hem turning. Pin pleats and
tack all around before finishing edges. These should be small and
evenly placed for an even weight distribution (fig 208).

CORNERS AND ANGLES OF HEMS
These are found on hems in upholstery or curtains and the front
edges of jackets; also skirts with a full-length opening.

Method: *The mitre*
1 Crease hems in fabric, then open fabric out and trim as in fig 209a.
2 Fold under small turnings on each hem and diagonal edge (fig
209b).
3 Fold back hems on to garment, secure at edge and oversew along
angle of corner also (fig 209c).

Hem finishes
For narrow hems (less than 1·5 cm) the following methods are
suitable:

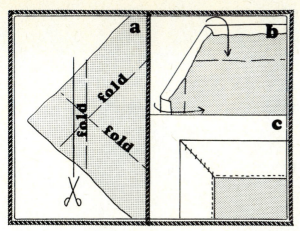

Figure 209

HAND STITCHED
1 Decide on hem width, then trim surplus to an even depth from hem edge.
2 Fold over fabric to ws of garment about 0·5 cm and press lightly (fig 210).
3 Fold over again to ws about 0·5 cm, or desired width of finished hem. Tack into place.

Figure 210   Figure 211

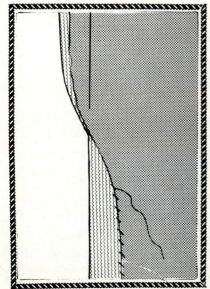
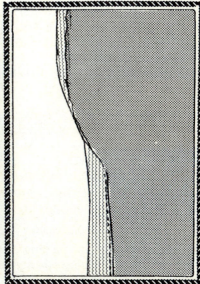

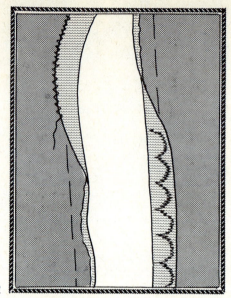

Figure 212

4 Secure with hemming, slip stitch or any other suitable hand stitch (see chapter 7). Remove tacks and press (fig 210).

ROLLED HEM (shell edged)
Suitable for soft or sheet fabrics. Use shell hemming by hand (see chapter 7) or machine using blind hemming stitch right over narrow turning.

MACHINED HEMS (quick method)

Method **A**: *Straight stitch*
1 Measure width of finished hem *plus* turnings and trim to this line, eg, a finished hem 1·5 cm *plus* 0·5 cm turnings, means cutting to 2 cm.
2 Turn under a narrow first turning. Press lightly.
3 Turn under a second turning to hem level. Pin and tack.
4 Remove pins, machine close to fold of turning. Remove tacks, press (fig 211).

Method **B**: *Zig-zag* (for swing needle and automatic machines)
Finish raw edge of turning with zig-zag before straight stitch machining into place. For a decorative hem edge on RS (narrow hems only) fold two turnings (or one, if fabric does not fray badly)

and tack into place. Zig-zag or use embroidery stitch over fold of turning using a stitch of a suitable width (fig 212).

Some machines will do blind hemming (a sewing machine equivalent to slip stitch) automatically after the dial positions are set correctly. The directions for your particular sewing machine will tell you which dials etc to change.

BOUND HEMS

There are four main types of bound hem. Two of these are not strictly what might be termed 'bound', but they do use bias or crossway binding to neaten, and one method uses a false binding made of the garment edge itself.

All are suitable for frayable fabrics, but method D is not suitable for any except a fairly straight hem, eg, jacket or sleeve edge.

Method A: Tailor's hem

1 Prepare hem, eg, cut to required depth, shrink to size etc, remembering that only *one* turning is needed.
2 Cut bias binding or crossway strip to length or circumference of hem edge (*plus* extra for joining).
3 Width of finished bind should be at least 0·5 cm, so cut strips 2 cm wide for 0·5 cm binding (see chapter 8 for cutting and joining crossway).
4 Prepare binding by pressing down one edge evenly towards the centre, WS in (fig 213a).
5 Position binding on to hem with raw edge of binding to raw edge of hem and RS of fabric together. Tack along creasemark (fig 213b).

Figure 213a, b, c

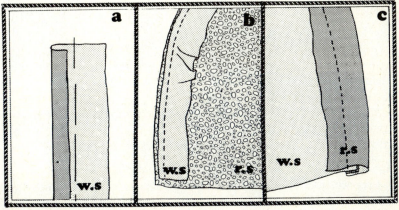

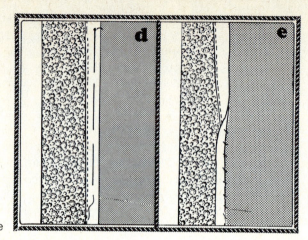

Figure 213d, e

6 Fold over edge of binding to enclose all raw edges (including edges of bind). Tack and machine through all thicknesses (fig 213c).
7 Tack bind to garment about 0·3 cm from fold (fig 213d).
8 Slip stitch to garment after folding back bind to line of tacks (fig 213e).

This stitch can be used on a hem without using a binding, providing edge of fabric is neatened first. Use stages 1 and 8. (See chapter 7, fig 86b.)

Method B: *Bound hem*, quick method
1 Trim edge of hem to actual length required as no turnings are to be made on this kind of hem.
2 Using a commercial or self-made binding (crossway strips) bind hem edge by same process as given for bound armhole edges (see chapter 20).

Method C: *Using a crossway binding*
Repeat stages 1–3 of method A.
4 Prepare binding by pressing both edges evenly towards centre (fig 214a).
5 Repeat stage 5 as for method A.
6 Keeping binding flat, but folding under remaining raw edge to creasemark, pin and tack into position (fig 214b). Hem or slip stitch to secure. Remove tacks. Press from ws of garment.

Method D: *French bind* (suitable only for straight edges)
1 Prepare hem edge and decide on width of finished bind, eg, a finished bind 1·5 cm wide will need a hem turning allowance of

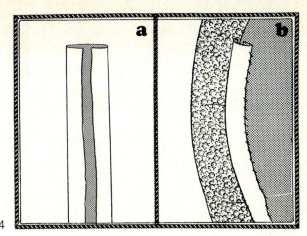

Figure 214

approximately 5–6 cm. The measurements given below will make a 1·5 cm bind.
2 Fold up turning to RS of garment. Pin and tack.
3 Machine stitch 1·5 cm away from fold all along hem edges (fig 215a).
4 Turn to WS and pull turning down so it is flat. Make a 0·75 cm turning along raw edge on to WS of fabric (fig 215b).
5 Take turning up on WS so that fold of binding edge meets machine stitching. Hem or slip stitch into place (fig 215c).

FACED HEMS (known as false hems)
Useful when you haven't quite enough fabric, or for a decorative

Figure 215

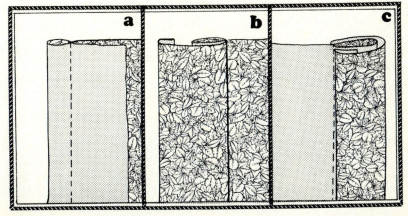

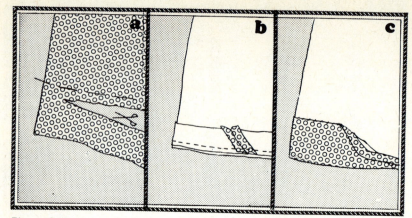

Figure 216

effect if made on to the RS of garment. The measurements given below are for a 5 cm facing.

Method
1 Mark off hem length on garment and add approximately 1·5 cm for a narrow turning allowance. Trim surplus fabric to this measurement (fig 216a).
2 Cut and join crossway strips (for curved or flared hems) or straight grain strips for straight hems, 8 cm wide (see chapter 19 for facings, chapter 8 for crossway strips).
3 Position facing to garment:
a with RS together for facing made on to WS.
b with WS together for facing made on to RS (showing).
Pin and tack 1·5 cm from raw edges (fig 216b).
4 Press facing over on to other side of garment. Press under 1·5 cm turning and secure facing to garment with hand or machine stitching (fig 216c).
Note: Special false hem bindings can be bought and applied as above; if using these make on to WS only.

Golden rules for hems
1 Remember that marking a hem usually needs two people (for a skirt or dress) unless you are fortunate enough to have a dressmaker's dummy (fig 217) of your identical shape and height. Hem markers can be used but some of these are not very accurate.

Figure 217

2 Measure hem level carefully when garment is on, wearing the same shoes and underclothes that you would normally be wearing with it.
3 Keep hem depth even, as unevenness will result in a badly hanging garment.
4 Choose correct size hem for fabric and position of hem on garment, eg, narrow hem for sleeves, wider hem for skirts, etc.
5 On transparent fabrics, keep first turning same depth as second for a neat effect.
6 Trim away excess fabric at corners and seams joins so they lie perfectly flat.
7 Choose correct hem finish for fabric, eg, bulky fabric looks clumsy with a double hem turning – better to have a bound, or edge-stitched turning.
8 Make a good, broad hem on skirt or dress, and a double hem on children's clothes. This will mean that hems can be let down at a later date if necessary.
9 A faced hem will give extra life to a garment which has become too short. Original hem can be let down and new hem faced with some other fabric.
10 Press all finished hems carefully, see Golden rules for pressing, chapter 24.

Words and terms used in this chapter (see Glossary for meanings)
Sewing terms

bias binding	straight grain	turning allowance
cross(way)	straight stitch	zig-zag
fray(able)		

General terms

calculated	diagonally	surplus
circumference	excess	transparent
commercial	identical	weight distribution
comparatively	parallel	

Things to do

1 State where you would use a binding on a hem. Give fabrics etc.
2 State where you would use a double folded hem. Give fabrics etc.
3 Do a sample piece of hemming using a hand stitch.
4 Do a sample piece of machine hemming. Check how this looks against your hand-stitched hem. Which looks best – on what fabrics?

PART SIX

The Professional Touch

Without the extra finishes which can make or mar clothes, a garment is likely to remain in the amateur category if it has been home made. The following items are not necessarily added last to a garment – indeed, in the case of pressing it is absolutely essential to press as you go – but they can give it that professional touch.

---

24. Pressing and Ironing

The chief part of successful dressmaking depends on whether you have pressed the garment properly at the various stages of making, and whether the final pressing was adequate. It cannot be emphasized enough, how important it is to **press each seam and join as you make it**; it is pressing which takes home dressmaking from the amateur, to the professional, standard. You have all seen home-sewn clothes with badly puckered seams and puffy hems. It seems such a shame that, for the sake of a few minutes at the ironing board, this could have been avoided.

One thing which should be made clear at this stage is that pressing does not mean ironing. *Ironing* is done merely by rubbing the iron up and down the fabric, with or without a cloth; *pressing* is done by holding the iron down on to the fabric for some seconds, with a dry or damp cloth between it and the fabric, then *lifting* it up and moving it along to the next place. Steam is really necessary for most pressing, whereas it isn't always necessary for ordinary ironing purposes.

Equipment

Irons: Be sure that the iron is light enough for you to handle easily as nothing is more tiring than an iron which feels as though it weighs two tons every time you lift it! (fig 218).

Ironing board or table: This should be of the right height for you to stand or sit at without giving you backache. It should be covered with a foam pad, then a clean cloth (fig 219).

Sleeve board: Useful for getting at sleeve seams and those places

Figure 218

Figure 219

which are too small to be put on the ironing board itself (fig 219).

Seam rolls: These are long, thin, cloth-covered rolls, looking rather like small draught excluders. They are used for pressing seams over and can be easily made by rolling up newspapers or magazines, covering with a thin layer of foam, then calico or heavy white cotton, stitched down tightly to hold in place (fig 220).

Tailor's hams: These are fat, ham-shaped, pressing aids which are used to press darts and curved areas. They can be of any size. (See fig 220.)

Pressing cloths: These you won't be able to do without. They are, next to the iron, the most essential part of pressing equipment. Wash out pressing cloths occasionally and always before using for the first time. Fine cotton for damp cloths, eg, muslin. Thin cottons for dry cloths.

Pressing fabrics and fibres
Cotton: Use a hot iron on ws of fabric. Damp cloth removes creases or folds (fig 221).

Linen: Very hot iron on ws of fabric (fig 221).

Wool: Use damp pressing cloth (if colourfast) and warm to moderate iron (fig 222). When pressing on RS of wool use a damp *and* a dry

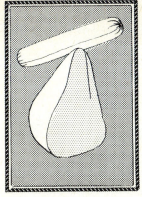

Figure 220   Figure 221

Figure 222

pressing cloth. If wool is scorched, rub quickly with some silver object, eg, a silver St Christopher, using a circular motion.

Silk: Iron when dry using warm iron on ws of fabric. Damp cloths can cause watermarking. Put layer of fabric between seam allowance and main fabric when pressing, to avoid seam marks occurring on RS (fig 223).

Rayons: Use cool to warm iron and press on ws. Never press on RS without using a cloth as this causes shine which may be impossible to remove (fig 223).

Nylon: If it needs pressing, do this gently on ws using cool to warm iron (fig 224).

Terylene: Very little ironing or pressing should be necessary. When pressing seams and darts, use cool to warm iron and damp pressing cloth (fig 224).

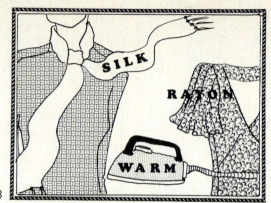

Figure 223

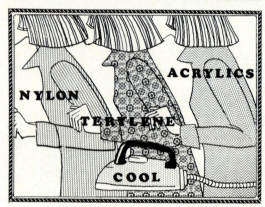

Figure 224

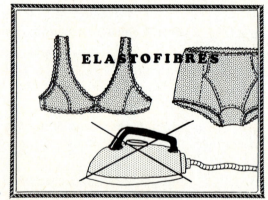

Figure 225

Acrylics: Use very cool iron and don't press over seams (causes marking). Use steam iron if possible, passing iron across fabric without actually touching it (fig 224).

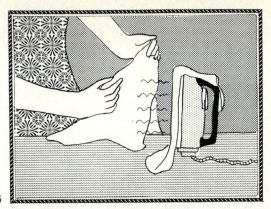

Figure 226

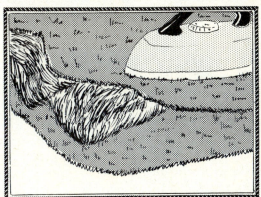

Figure 227

Elastofibres, eg, 'Spanzelle', 'Lycra': Do not press or iron (fig 225).

Laminates, eg, PVC: Do not press or iron, use hammer or wooden mallet to flatten seams when making up.

Special fabrics
Velvet, pile or napped fabrics
Fold thick terry towel in half, place velvet or pile fabric on to this, face down and press gently. Alternatively, stand iron upright on table, put damp cloth over iron and pass your garment fabric gently to and fro in front of steam, which should penetrate the fabric (fig 226).

Stretch fabrics: Only press seams (on ws), being careful not to stretch any part during pressing.

Fur fabrics: Use thick terry towels if two furry edges are to be pressed, eg, faced edges or hems. Place fur between them (fig 227).

Knitted fabrics: Use a damp cloth on wrong side. Press way of rib.

Golden rules for ironing

When caring for your clothes:

1 Iron double parts on both sides.
2 Iron along selvedge threads (warp threads).
3 Iron fabric on ws for a dull finish.

Golden rules for pressing

When making your clothes:

1 To press hems, place piece of fabric under edge of hem before stitching hem down. Press edge of hem *over* this piece of fabric, then remove before stitching. This gives a neat, pressed edge without pressing marks showing on RS of hem.

2 When using seam roll, place roll under seams (to RS) and press over roll on ws.

3 Use tailor's hams, curved end of sleeveboard or seam roll when pressing curved parts or darts. Place fabric so point of dart fits over fat part of ham in a gentle curve. Press well.

4 Don't press over pins or tacks – these may cause marking. (The only exception is tacks holding pleats down; use a fine thread such as Coats' Drima and to prevent marking tack only along bottom and top.)

5 Test heat of iron on piece of same fabric before using on garment.

6 Press on ws of work if possible. If pressing from from RS place dry pressing cloth between damp pressing cloth and fabric to avoid watermarking on RS.

7 If fabric is not pre-shrunk, shrink it before making up and before pressing (see chapter 5, under Shrinking).

8 Lift iron up and down, *not* from side to side.

9 Press darts before side seams, side seams before hems. For darts which are not cut open, first press stitching line then press dart to one side. Press tucks in same manner.

10 For seams on really heavy fabrics, first damp with sponge then rub point of iron along them (put cloth between first), then press as normal.

11 If press mark shows, remove by holding fabric over steam (don't scald yourself!).

12 Do not leave iron on ironing board cover, face down – it will burn! Leave on asbestos or metal holder.

13 *Switch off iron at mains when finished.*

Words and terms used in this chapter (see Glossary for meanings)
Sewing terms

seam rolls	selvedge	tailor's hams

General terms

adequate	penetrate	sequence
amateur	scorch(ed)	

Things to do
1 Explain the difference between ironing and pressing.
2 Press some different kinds of fabric scraps, noting temperatures of iron and reaction of fabrics.
3 Make a list of the right times to press the garment you are making now.

◎ ◎ ◎

25. Pockets

'Lucy Locket lost her pocket', which may have meant she hadn't sewn it on properly, although in those days pockets could be rather like small dolly bags attached to a dress by strings or ribbons.

Pockets nowadays are just as popular as ever, even on skintight trousers where there isn't room for a pocket at the hip or backside. In this case pockets are often placed lower, on the knees or thighs.

Again the choice of pocket style much depends on the style of the garment and also the fabric. Patch pockets go well with most styles, and can be adapted to work well with most fabrics. Some of the nicest patch pockets are those found on 'safari' type jackets or shirts; these often have a centre pleat and a button-down flap.

Pockets with zips set at a slant on jackets are very useful for storing wallets or tucking cold hands into on a wintry day. The choice of pocket style is yours but be guided by commonsense as well as fashion.

Patch pockets
Definition: A shaped piece of material neatened and stitched flat on to garment with one edge left open and neatened.

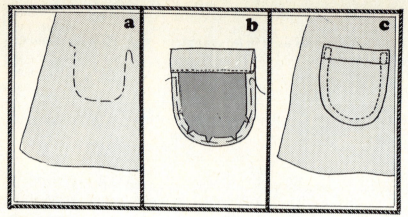

Figure 228

Method

1 Make up garment section.

2 Decide where pockets are to be placed and tack a line around this position (fig 228a).

3 Cut pocket to desired shape and size, add turnings.

4 Neaten one edge with binding, facing, self-hem, etc (fig 228b).

5 Turn under the remaining raw edges to ws. Tack in place, clipping any curves or angles (fig 228b).

6 Position pocket on garment over tacking line. Pin and tack around three edges.

7 Machine close to folded edge all round, leaving top open for opening. Start and finish with a box-shape or triangle of stitching for extra strength at opening (fig 228c).

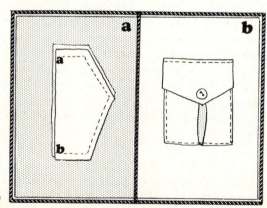

Figure 229

Patch pockets can be interfaced for a neater, crisper look.

PATCH POCKETS WITH A BOX PLEAT

The method of making is exactly the same as for an ordinary patch pocket but allow extra for the pleat when cutting out, and make up pleat before turning under raw edges of pocket. For inverted pleats follow same procedure. (For pleats see chapter 11.)

PATCH POCKETS WITH A FLAP

Make up patch pocket and apply to garment. Cut two flaps for each pocket, same length as pocket top plus turnings, by width required (centre can be shaped to a point).

Method

1 Placing RS together, stitch upper and underflap from **a** to **b**. Clip angles. Layer seams and press (fig 229a).
2 Turn through to RS. Turn raw edges in on remaining side. Tack down close to edge.
3 Position flap 1·5 cm above opening of pocket. Pin and tack in place.
4 Remove pins. Machine close to edge making sure all raw edges are enclosed and ends are secure (fig 229b).
5 Flap can be fastened with press studs or buttons if wished.

ROUND POCKET WITH A ZIP (fig 230)

Method

1 Cut paper pattern to size of circle required (for guide draw round a saucer or tea plate). Then cut through centre. This gives you two halves of pocket.
2 Cut fabric pieces from paper pattern, allowing at least 1·5 cm turnings all round, including straight edges (fig 231a).
3 Fold under seam allowance to WS all way round each section and tack down. Using slip hemming or overcasting stitch (see chapter 7), join straight edges together on WS of work, 1·5 cm from each end of pocket opening only (depending on size of pocket). Trim raw edges of circle to about 0·5 cm from fold (fig 231b).
4 Measure length of opening and buy a lightweight zip to fit this measurement exactly. Place zip under opening. Pin and tack in place as close to folded edge as possible without hindering free movement of zip (fig 231c).
5 Remove pins. Machine on tacking using a zipper foot attachment. Remove tacks in zip and press on WS.

Figure 230

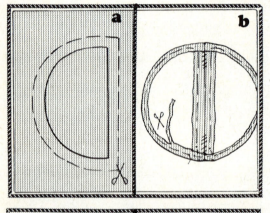

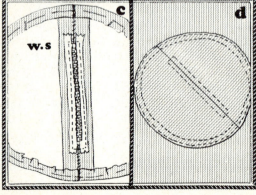

Figure 231

6 Close zip. Position pocket on garment. Zips can be placed horizontal, sideways or on diagonal. Tack in place.
7 Machine close to fold all round circle edge. Machine again about 0·5 cm from first line; this will enclose all raw edges (fig 231d).

BOUND POCKET
The method for making a bound pocket is very much the same as for making a bound buttonhole (see chapter 14, Fastenings). Pieces of fabric cut for making the pocket should be long enough to make the bind *and* the pocket back and front, eg, a pocket 12 cm wide × 15 cm deep needs a strip 16 cm × 26 cm.

Method
1 Mark position of pocket opening on garment with line of tacking.
2 Lay pocket section over marked place, RS together and centralizing it. Pin and tack (fig 232a).
3 Machine a rectangle round line of tacking, marking pocket opening, about 0·5 cm all round (fig 232a).
4 Cut along tacking line through both thicknesses, snipping diagonally into corners (fig 232a).
5 Press seams open and two triangles back (fig 232b).
6 Pull pocket through opening until it lies flat on WS, making an inverted pleat over both seams. Press and baste (see chapter 7, Hand Stitches) edges together diagonally to hold it temporarily (fig 232c).
7 Turn to RS of work and backstitch along two seam lines through all the thicknesses (fig 232d).
8 Pull down upper to lower pocket and tack two pieces together so they lie flat. Cut away excess fabric on lower pocket section (fig 232e).
9 Machine stitch outer edges of pocket and neaten if they fray. Remove tacking (fig 232e).
10 Fold back garment fabric and machine across each triangle through all thicknesses (fig 232f).

WELT AND FLAP POCKETS
These are similar to a bound pocket except that some have a flap above pocket opening and some have a flap (welt) below pocket opening. They are used most often on suits and coats.

Cut flaps same length as the pocket opening, *plus* 1 cm, plus turnings × twice width required, *plus* turnings, eg, for 5 cm wide flap to fit opening 10 cm long cut fabric 13 cm × 14 cm (1·5 cm turnings).

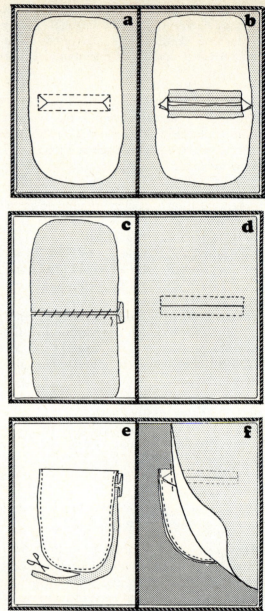

Figure 232

Method
1 Fold welt (flap) section in half lengthways, RS inside. Tack and

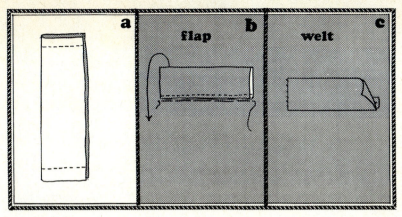

Figure 233

machine on fitting line at each end. Remove tacks, clip angles, layer seams and press (fig 233a).

2 Turn through to RS and press again.

3 Mark position of pocket with line of tacking on garment.

4 Lay RS of *welt* to RS garment below pocket markings with raw edges on tacked line (fig 233c) or lay RS of *flap* to RS garment above pocket markings with raw edges on tacked line (fig 233b).

5 Complete as for bound pockets.

6 Press welt up and slip stitch in place (fig 233c). Press flap downwards (fig 233b).

Golden rules for pockets

1 Make sure that pockets are in correct position on pattern to achieve a good balance. Once material is cut and garment made up (eg, bound or welt pockets) it is very difficult to readjust. A coat pattern I used many years ago had welt pockets about knee level – fine for monkeys – no good otherwise!

2 Allow enough material of same fabric to make pockets or choose a contrasting colour or texture fabric of a similar weight.

3 Mark off position of pockets with a line of pins or tacking and try garment on to see if any adjustments need to be made.

4 For pockets which are inserted or inset, do make sure they are big enough for the hand to go in. Patch pockets can be any size according to where they are placed, eg, tiny patch pockets on sleeves are fine for train tickets etc.

5 Cut pockets on straight grain or true cross.

6 Place pockets where they can be reached conveniently (but not

by thieves). If they are on an outer garment, make them with some kind of fastening to avoid loss of belongings.

Words and terms used in this chapter (see Glossary for meanings)
Sewing terms

bound pocket	fray	patch pocket
box pleat	interface(d)	seam allowance
clip angles	inverted pleat	welt pocket
clip curves		

General terms

adapt(ed)	diagonal(ly)	rectangle
centralizing	excess	temporarily
contrast(ing)	horizontal	triang(le)(ular)

Things to do
1 State where you might use patch pockets and give reasons.
2 Design and draw a new pocket style. Give method of making up.
3 State where you might use a bound slit type pocket.
4 Suggest where you might use pockets other than on garments and give uses etc.

◎ ◎ ◎

26. Belts

Belts can give a completely different line to a dress or jacket by emphasizing the contours of the body; they can accentuate a seam line or shape; or they can give a touch of interest to an otherwise plain outfit, eg, a belt of coloured knotted scarves, or a soft suede belt around a tweedy wool coat, can look superb.

Belts made of material usually fall into one of three categories:
1 Soft-tie.
2 Semi-stiffened.
3 Very stiff (sometimes these are shaped too).

Method for making a soft-tie belt
1 Cut piece of fabric on straight grain, length required for finished belt (*plus* turnings) × twice width of finished belt (*plus* 1·5 cm

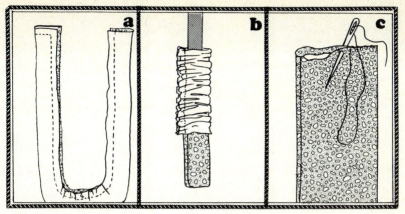

Figure 234

turnings), eg, a 2 m long belt × 2·5 cm wide will require fabric 2·030 m long × 8 cm wide.

2 Placing RS and raw edges together, pin and tack 1·5 cm from raw edges all along one long side and across one short side (fig 234a).

3 Remove pins and machine on tacking line. Remove tacks, press. Snip off angles etc.

4 Using a pencil or knitting needle (blunt end) push belt through to RS, starting at machined end (fig 234b).

5 Turn in raw ends and oversew firmly (fig 234c). Press belt lightly. The belt can be machined close to edge all round if required.

Method for semi-stiffened belts
Made as for soft belts but having an interlining or interfacing of some kind which is fairly soft (see chapter 9, Interfacings) stitched in or ironed on before making up belt. (See corded rouleau, chapter 8, Crossway.)

Method for stiffened belts
These are usually made to take a lot of wear or to look crisp and tailored.

1 Cut belt from fabric.

2 Cut stiffening to fit exactly, ie, only one thickness is used and no turning allowances are necessary.

3 Make up belt as for a soft-tie belt but omit stitching one end.

4 When belt is turned through to RS, push stiffened backing or interfacing through belt until it fits. Turn in remaining raw edge and oversew firmly.

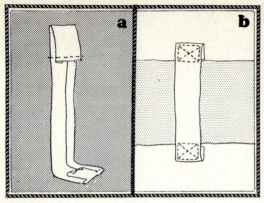

Figure 235

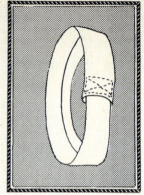

Figure 236

Belt carriers

These can be made on the garment itself or separately for slotting a belt back on to itself and holding in place.

Method: Handworked
Make exactly as for large handworked eye or buttonloop (see chapter 14, Fastenings). Large stitches are taken across garment to fit belt, and buttonhole or loop stitch is then worked from end to end across these stitches (see chapter 7, Hand Stitches).

Method: Fabric made, type **A**
1 Cut strips of fabric on straight grain, length required *plus* 3 cm for turnings × twice width plus turnings. Remember to allow 1·5 cm extra at each end for sewing down, eg, a belt carrier length for a 5 cm wide belt should be about 11 cm long × 6 cm wide (1·5 cm turnings) giving finished width of 1·5 cm.
2 Place RS and raw edges together along length. Machine (2 cm from fold if finished width of belt carrier is to be 2 cm wide, 1·5 cm from fold if it is to be 1·5 cm wide and so on). Trim raw edges to slightly less than finished width. Turn through to RS.
3 Turn under raw edges at each end. Tack across and trim away surplus fabric on underneath section (fig 235a).
4 Place on garment. Machine down at each end using box shape and diagonal stitching (fig 235b).

Method: Free carrier, type **B**
Repeat as for type **A** to end of stage 2.
Fold in raw edges at one end and press. Slot in raw edges of other end into this opening. Stitch in place (fig 236).

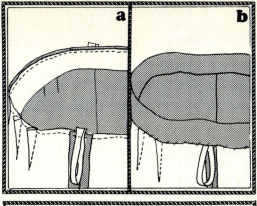

Figure 237

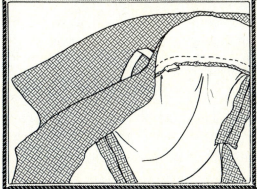

Figure 238

Hanging loops
These are made on skirts, trousers, coats, etc, so that they can be hung up without making marks on the garment.

*Method **A**: For trousers and skirts*
1 Before placing waistband in position, attach two (equal length) tapes, each folded in half, at side seams (fig 237a).
2 Finish off waistband, enclosing raw edges of tape (fig 237b).

*Method **B**: For coats and jackets*
Make these as you would a fabric belt carrier (type **A**) and either attach after making up garment to neck edge, or insert between collar and facing, before applying facing (fig 238).

Golden rules for belts etc
1 Belt should be big enough to go round waist, hips or wherever, and fasten without constricting breathing or circulation. Tight

belts may give you a wasp waist but heaven help your digestive processes!

2 Cut fabric belts on straight grain or true cross (straight grain only for soft-tie belts).

3 Make carriers on garments so belts don't get lost. Make free carrier for belt to slot into (makes it lie flat).

4 Carriers should be big enough to take belts without rucking up.

5 Put hanging loops at waists of skirts and trousers; shoulders of sleeveless dresses (attach between main part and facing at neck edge) and necks of jackets, and coats. Loops can be renewed if they get worn, but sections of garment can't be.

Words and terms used in this chapter (see Glossary for meanings)
Sewing terms

belt carrier	interfacing	tailor(ed)
clip angles	interlining	true cross
fitting line	layer seams	turning allowance
hanging loops	straight grain	

General terms

accentuate	contrast(ing)	omit
categories	diagonals	surplus
contour(s)	emphasiz(ing)	

Things to do

1 Design three styles of belt. Give methods for making up.

2 State where you would put hanging loops, and what you would make them from.

◎   ◎   ◎

27. Trimmings

Even the plainest, most simple designs can be given an exciting look by the imaginative use of trimmings. There are so many kinds of trimming on the market today that the choice is almost unlimited.

Some really marvellous effects can be obtained, combining the various types of timmings. Search upholstery and lampshade trimming departments as well as the general haberdashery ones,

Figure 239

as some really interesting textured trimmings can be found on these. Make sure all the trimmings are washable or dry cleanable if you want to be able to clean them or the garment they are on. Mixtures of the right trimmings can give an 'ethnic' feel to plain outfits – as the gypsy look in fig 239.

Lace

Edging lace: This has one plain edge and one shaped edge and is made for applying to edges of garments.

Insertion lace: This has two plain straight edges. It is intended for applying on to garments or for insertion into seams etc.

APPLYING EDGING LACE

Method **A**

1 Fold over a turning of 0·5 cm on to RS of garment at edge. Press well.

2 Place lace edging so straight edge of lace is level with raw edge of garment (on RS). Tack and machine into place using straight stitch or zig-zag (fig 240).

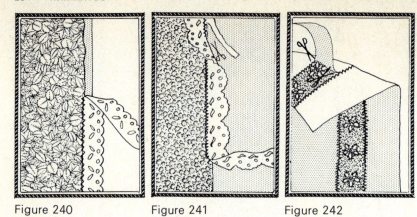

Figure 240   Figure 241   Figure 242

Method **B**
Trim edge to be neatened evenly all along. Place straight edge of
lace slightly above this raw edge on to RS and tack in place. Set
machine to satin stitch or narrow zig-zag and machine along,
enclosing lace edge. On back of the garment or article, trim away
excess fabric down to machine stitching (fig 241).

Method for applying insertion lace
1 Position lace on to fabric and tack to hold (down the centre).
2 Set machine to zig-zag or satin stitch and machine down each
side of lace, enclosing the edges. (Straight stitch can be used if
fabric is to be left uncut behind lace.)
3 For a lacey look, cut away excess fabric behind lace, close to
machine stitching. Be very careful not to cut lace (fig 242).

JOINING LACE
Joins in lace can be made invisibly by overlapping one piece on to
another, tacking down to hold. The lace motif (pattern) is used as a
guide for stitching along. Use either a hand stitch (oversewing or
blanket stitch) or a machine stitch (zig-zag or satin stitch). When
threads have been fastened off securely at each end, cut away
excess lace at back of work close to stitching (fig 243).

Ribbon and braid
Depending on the type of ribbon (whether it is already embroidered)
and the width (narrow kinds need only one line of machining),
machine into place on the garment or article, using a straight stitch
or any swing needle stitches. Embroidery stitches made in a

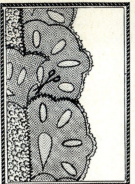
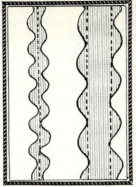

Figure 243   Figure 244   Figure 245

contrasting colour thread look especially good holding down a
ribbon to a hem. If the ribbon is very wide, two rows of stitching
will be needed, each row as close to the edge of ribbon as possible.
Keep machining even (use edge of presser foot as a guide, see chapter
6). Always tack ribbon down first or pin in place with pins at right
angles to ribbon. (A machine can pass easily over pins if they are put
in this way.) Make sure ribbon is pre-shrunk first if garment or
article is to be washed.

RIC-RAC BRAID
This is a wavy braid which is popular for trimming children's
clothes and casual garments. It is also fairly inexpensive compared
to other trimmings. Use a single row of straight stitch machining
down centre of braid to hold in place. For very wide ric-rac, over
1·5 cm, use two rows of machining (fig 244).

Tassels and fringing
Usually these have a straight section at one edge which is applied
to garment or article. Single tassels can be sewn on by hand using
very firm stitches. For tassel fringing machine one row of straight
stitching on edge.

Patchwork appliqué (shop bought)
For those people who cannot make their own appliqué designs,
there are various kinds available commercially. Some of these are
iron-on (for the really lazy – and quite often they fall off at the first
wash!) and some are meant to be stitched on. When stitching them
on, use a good firm hand stitch (hemming or backstitch) or a machine

straight stitch. If the edges look a bit raw or fraying, use a blanket or buttonhole hand stitch, or a machine zig-zag or satin stitch, to attach them. Make sure they are colourfast before applying – that goes for all trimmings (fig 245). For stitches see chapter 7; for bindings, pipings, etc, see chapters 20, 21.

Words and terms used in this chapter (see Glossary for meanings)
Sewing terms

| appliqué | haberdashery department | zig-zag |
| edging lace | insertion lace | |

General terms

| excess | motif |
| indication | texture(d) |

Things to do
1 Design a dress using two or more types of trimming. Give fabric choice, colours, etc.
2 Give instances of where you would use insertion lace. Make a drawing to show where.

◎ ◎ ◎

28. Accessory after the Fact

'Accessories' means belts, shoes, boots, bags, hats, scarves, gloves, jewellery, and all those extras which turn items of clothing into an outfit. Accessories can make or mar: the most beautiful clothes can look a mess if they are worn with ill-matched or scruffy accessories. On the other hand, simple inexpensive clothes can look fabulous dollied up with some well-chosen accessories.

FOOTWEAR (fig 246)
Try to buy the best you can afford. The best is not necessarily the most expensive or the latest fashion gimmick. Buy well-fitting, good quality leather or suede (or synthetic fabrics if they allow the skin to 'breathe') with the uppers stitched to the sole as well as stuck (they wear better) and a fairly thick leather or crêpe sole and

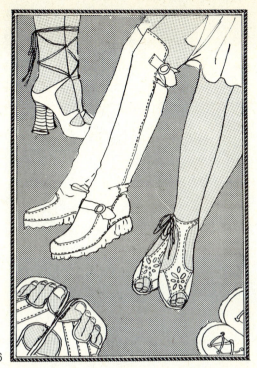

Figure 246

heel (leather soles should be at least 0·3 cm thick if they are to last –
put on a rubber stick-on sole if they are thinner). Cork is not good
for anything other than sandals as it breaks down too easily.

Make sure footwear looks clean and keep boots and shoes in tip-
top condition when they are not being worn, by stuffing rolled up
newspaper in the foot part. Rolled magazines in the legs of boots
helps them to retain their shape. Spray footwear with rain pro-
tector to make them mark, and rain, proof – rub 'Vaseline' over
patent leather shoes each time after wearing them and never dry
them in front of a fire (allow them to dry naturally to prevent
cracking). If you cannot get rid of scuff marks on shoes with a damp
sponge or polish, touch them up with matching colour shoe dye.
Sprinkle talcum powder in shoes occasionally to keep them smelling
sweet.

BAGS (fig 247)
This means all kinds of bags, from canvas or denim tote bags (the
large hold-all kind) to the best leather and suede handbags. You

Figure 247

don't need a bag for every outfit, but aim to have one for general use (make yourself a fabric one). You need one for carrying lots of things (again, easy to make from fabric) and perhaps a leather one for best, in a neutral colour. Keep them looking smart, dust fabric bags with a stiff brush occasionally and wash them now and again if the fabric allows this. Protect leather bags with waterproofing Aerosol spray and polish sometimes.

BELTS (fig 248)
This can mean anything from leather thonging to scarves or bead ropes knotted together. Imagination can work wonders. Try the following ideas or adapt them.

TIE BELTS
1 Plait three long, fine scarves together. Knot at each end if wished.
2 Twist a rope of beads around a long scarf. Secure at each end with a few stitches.

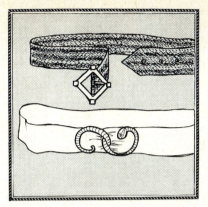

Figure 248   Figure 249

3 Cut or buy strips of leather thonging. Plait together or thread large wooden beads on, every so often.

BUCKLE OR CLASP BELTS

1 Make a belt from canvas webbing; attach buckle at one end and make eyelets at the other.
2 Make a soft suede belt and add a scout's 's' clasp to it, or stitch a row of buttons one end and a row of loops to match, at the other.

SCARVES (fig 249)

Buy one a month and this way you will get a range of patterns and colours which can entirely alter the look of an outfit. Try these ideas:
1 With natural or camel coloured trousers and sweater, knot fine silk scarf (in colour of your choice) at neck, adding a rope of plain wooden beads to match.
2 Wear a printed long skirt and a cotton shirt knotted under bust, with a man's cotton paisley-printed scarf (or hankie) tied around the head and knotted at back of neck. The addition of hooped earrings make this a stunning look.
3 With a plain dark evening outfit (trousers or skirt) and no jewellery, liven things up by knotting a long silk or chiffon scarf around the head, letting the ends trail over one ear 'silent movie Queen' style.

HATS (fig 250)

My favourite accessory – I've got lots and haven't the courage to

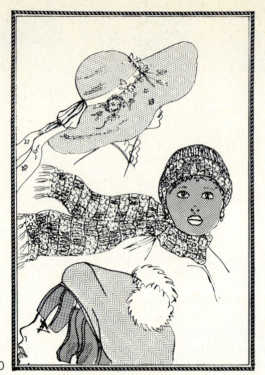

Figure 250

wear any of them! You may fare better. Try these ideas:

1 Large brimmed straw hat. Tie a scarf round crown letting ends float free at back, or sew on lots of artificial flowers on crown or brim.

2 Crochet and knitted 'pull-ons' in stripes or plain, with long scarves to match wound round and round the neck. Wear with casual clothes. Made in sparkly Lurex threads they look great for evening.

3 Flat beanies (berets): Go mad with bright colours and add pompons, patches or tassels.

JEWELLERY AND EXTRAS

Fake fur or feathers to throw round the neck, in crazy colours; big beads or chunky jewellery in very obvious plastic; flowers in artificial colours that Nature never intended; fun gimmicks to go mad with as they need not cost a lot. Try these:

1 Add a fake flower above one ear – a touch of the exotic for parties (fig 251).

Figure 251

2 Add a detachable fur collar and cuffs (needn't be real fur) to a cable knit or ribbed woollen jumper for a posh 'my daddy is a millionaire' look.
3 Add suede elbow patches and yoke to a woollen or corduroy jacket – an inexpensive touch of luxury.

Swop accessories (except footwear) with friends, or pool them with a group so there is more to choose from. Stock up on ribbons, trimmings, unusual belts and button fastenings. Make lots of things like bags and hats. Above all have fun dressing up. Clothes may not 'maketh man' but they maketh the most of many women!

Words and terms used in this chapter (see Glossary for meanings)
General terms

adapt	exotic	retain
Aerosol spray	luxury	scuff
beanies	neutral	synthetic
canvas webbing	paisley print	thonging

Things to do
1 Make up some ideas for accessories, listing them under 'sensible – won't date quickly' and 'gimmicks – fun but fast out of fashion'.
2 Translate some of these ideas into actual things, eg, make up the belt or whatever it is, noting how much material it takes and cost in comparison to shop prices.

Glossary

It is important to know how this glossary is meant to be used. At the end of each of the preceding chapters you will see a list of sewing terms and general terms that may cause difficulty through unfamiliarity. These are listed again alphabetically below, together with a short, simple explanation of their meaning in the context of this book.

Only the meanings that are relevant to the text are given here and if you want to know any extra meanings you can look them up in an ordinary dictionary.

absorbent Soaks up moisture

accelerator The pedal which makes a machine go faster.

accent(s) Touch of colour or design feature which emphasizes the finished effect.

accentuate To emphasize or underline something

access A way of entering

accommodate Allow, enable

accurate Exact, perfectly correct

acrylics A group of synthetic fibres, eg, *Acrilan, Orlon, Courtelle,* etc.

adapt(ed) Alter an idea to suit another purpose

adequate Enough, sufficient

adjustable Changeable, movable

Aerosol spray Tiny drops of a substance, compressed in a can, making a high-pressure spray.

all-over pattern A pattern which is printed all over the fabric in various directions, not having an upright way.

alternative(ly) A different way, a choice

amateur A beginner or non-professional

angular With corners, and angles or sharp edges – if applied as a descriptive term to people, usually means they have a squarish build with prominent bones.

applicable Appropriate to

application When something is applied to something else.

appliqué A method of embroidery where one piece of fabric is put to another, usually of different colour, or pattern and stitched down.

approximately Nearly, about

artificial False, not real

Art Nouveau A style of art and design, popular recently, but originated in the 19th century by artists such as William Morris, Dante Gabriel Rossetti, Aubrey Beardsley, etc.

askew Twisted to one side

bacteria Very small one-celled organisms which grow mainly in damp places on animal or vegetable matter.

balance points (marks) The marks or notches on a pattern which should be transferred to the fabric; these marks must be matched on joining garment sections so that they fit together.

bale A roll of fabric

basting Another word for tacking; often meaning diagonal or slanted tacks.

beanies Berets, small felt hats

belt carrier The loop of thread or fabric which holds belt to main garment.

bias Cut at any angle from the straight grain

bias binding A binding which is cut on the true cross, with two turnings permanently creased down as a guide to use.

bizarre Weird, very unusual

blindhemming A method of machining, where stitches do not show on RS of work.

bobbin (spool) The sewing machine part that has the lower thread wound on it; it fits into a case found under the needle plate, known as the bobbin case.

bodice The top section of the garment from the waist to the neck (omitting the sleeves).

bodkin A blunt-ended, large-eyed tool for threading elastic etc

bolls The fluffy seed heads of the cotton plant

bound pocket A pocket which has the opening bound with fabric to neaten the raw edges; the material of the main garment covers the pocket which is made from extra pieces of fabric hidden underneath.

box pleat Two knife pleats facing away from each other (see pleats)

budget To work out a system of saving (or spending) money

bulk(y) Large, clumsy, thick

calculate(d) Work(ed) out, estimate(d)

calculation A sum, an estimated amount

canvas webbing A coarsely woven jute or hessian braid which is used for carpets, upholstery, etc.

carded Raked over with a comb-shaped tool; performed on wool, cotton, etc, to remove impurities and smooth out fibres.

categories Groups

casing A holder for elastic etc

cellulosic fibres Fibres of vegetable origin, eg, cotton

centimetre (cm) A unit of metric measurement; 100th of a metre.

centraliz(ed)(ing) Put in middle

channel seam One which has an extra piece of fabric placed underneath the fitting line.

chevron A diagonal pointed pattern, with the stripes of each part making a 'v' shape.

circumference The measurement of the outer edge, usually of a circle

clip angles Make a notch into an inner angle, or cut across diagonally so that when angle is turned through to RS, it will lie flat.

clip curves Clip 'v' shaped notches into curved seams and turnings so they lie properly.

clip seam As above

clockwise Going round in the same direction as the hands of a clock.

close weave The threads in a fabric are lying close together in both directions (warp and weft).

cocoon The casing the silkworm makes itself to prepare for meta-morphosis, ie, when it comes out as a moth.

coincide Coming at the same time; meeting.

colour contrasts Where extra colours are added – completely different or at variance to the first.

colour shades Colours to which a dark pigment has been added making them of various brightness or drabness.

colour tones The degrees or depth of colour

commercial Shop bought; available in a shop

comparatively In comparison to something else

components Ingredients, the parts making up something.

concealed Hidden

conspicuous Showing, obvious (when used in sewing means showing on RS).

construction The making up of something or putting it together.

continuous In one long length; sometimes joined to form a circle.

contour(ing) Outline, curves, etc

contrasting Different from what is already there to an obvious degree.

conversely On the other hand, oppositely

conversion Change over

co-ordinates Matched separates which blend and harmonize (clothes which can be worn together without looking ill-matched).

cord(ing) Tubular or rope-like cotton suitable for padding or filling etc

corded seam A seam which has been padded with cord to make it stand out.

corresponding Matching up to

cotton linters Pieces of cotton fibre

cross(way) Any fabric cut on the true cross, ie, cut at exact 45° angle from the straight grain.

crotch seams The back and front seams of trousers which go from between legs to centre of waist.

measurement See page 24

curb Cut down, prevent

dart(s)(ed) A fold taken into material with one or more pointed ends, stitched along through two thicknesses but not stitched down to main fabric.

detachable Being able to be removed or taken off

diagonally At an angle from the vertical or horizontal; quite often in sewing, an angle of 45°.

diameter The measurement from one point to another (usually across the middle of a circle).

discriminating Choosing wisely

distinctive Stands out from background

distribu(ted)(tion) Parcelled out, spread about

double-stitched seam Made as an open seam to start, then one seam turning trimmed to half width of other. Larger half is folded over first and both are stitched down to main garment.

double top stitched seam An ordinary open seam which is top stitched at an even width parallel to the fitting line on both sides.

drape Hanging in soft folds; only soft materials do this.

drastic(ally) Serious measure taken as a last resort usually

dropped sleeveline One where shoulder seam is extended beyond the point of the natural shoulderline over crown part of upperarm.

easing Pushing in gently, to make one part fit another of a smaller size.

edging lace Lace with one plain edge and one fancy edge.

efficient Competent, capable of doing good work.

emphasiz(e)(ing) Making something stand out from its background.

encounter Meet, come across

entails Means, involves

estimate Roughly work out or calculate

ethnic Of different race, country or culture

excess Extra amount

exotic Unusual, perhaps with foreign or Southern flavour, eg, a South Sea Island look would be exotic.

extend Make longer or larger

extrovert Having a lively personality; one who is sociable and outward going.

facings Pieces of fabric laid over the main garment and seamed at the edges; a method of neatening edges.

factors Influential facts

false hems Sometimes known as faced or artificial hems; made by adding a facing to the hem edge.

fell The width of a finished seam

felt(ing) Matting together of fibres

fibres The tiniest parts of yarn or thread, thin and hairlike

fibrous Made of fibres loosely packed

figure type This is the description of body shape based on height.

fitting line Also known as pattern or stitching line; the actual line where machining would come, for seams, darts, edges, etc.

forefinger The first finger of each hand

fraction(ally) Small distance or measurement from; less than one unit.

fray(able)(ability) This means that the cut ends of a fabric start to unravel.

French seam The seam is joined as an open seam first (ws tog.) at half width of seam allowance; fabric is then turned to other side and folded down at seam and another row of stitching is made along seam on fitting line.

function(al) Having a useful purpose

garish Bright to the point of looking terrible

gather(ed)(ing) A means of reducing fullness; running stitch or large machine stitch is made in the fabric and pulled up to make the piece smaller.

gimmick Trendy fashion which is only new for a short time and will attract a lot of attention for that period.

haberdashery department The department of a shop which sells all the extras needed for needlework, eg, pins, tape measures, needles, ribbons, etc.

hanging loops The loops which are stitched to garments to hang them up by.

horizontal Sideways

identically Exactly the same

imitation A copy

inconspicuous Hidden; made on to the ws; not showing.

incorporate(d) Included in

indication A sign of

influenced Affected by something or someone

insertion lace A lace trimming with two straight edges

instruction manual Book of rules and guidance, eg, for using a machine.

interfac(e)(ing) To back a section of fabric with another piece of fabric or to give it body or to prevent it stretching.

interlin(e)(ing) Same as the above but possibly using a lining fabric rather than an interfacing fabric.

intertwine Twist two or more (threads) together

intimidated Frightened by

introvert Opposite of extrovert, a shy, withdrawn personality

inverted pleat Two knife pleats facing towards each other (see pleats).

jaundice(d) Looking yellow; comes from 'jaundice' which is a disease that can make skin and eyes look yellow.

kimono sleeve One which is cut all in one with the bodice or which has the top fold of the sleeve in line with the shoulder seam (the natural shoulderline is lowered and the sleeve is large and squared off).

laminated Layers (of fabric) put together; one may have a plasticized surface, eg, PVC.

latter When two or more things are mentioned it means the last of these.

layer seams Trim down each layer of the seam turnings so that they come one above the other in steps; layering helps to make the seam lie flat.

layout When the pattern is placed on the material ready for cutting out.

lining(s) Pieces of fabric joined in the same way as the garment and attached to the inside of the garment to neaten it; also gives the garment body, or prevents the fabric being see-through.

located Situated, found, placed

logical Reasonable, sensible, step by step

lustre A shiny surface

luxury A special item which either costs a lot of money or is very rare.

magyar sleeve Has the underarm seam going in a straight line or a smooth line from wrist (or sleeve hem) to waist; no armhole seam.

manipulate Handle something, altering it to suit oneself.

manual Book of instructions, handbook

manually By hand

mediocre Middling, not very interesting

metamorphosis The process of changing from one thing to another, eg, a silkworm into a moth.

metre (m) A unit of measurement (length, width); 100 cm = 1 metre.

metric system The method of using metres, centimetres, etc, for measurement.

mildew A fungal (mushroom-like) organism which attacks fibres and rots them; it lives in damp conditions.

mineral An ore which comes from the ground and contains metal in one form or another.

miscellaneous Odds and ends, various, assortments

motif Recurring pattern or theme

mounting Backing garment sections with lining fabric before joining them together; see Interlining.

nap Surface depth on a fabric, rather hairy or downy with hairs (if long enough) being brushed in one direction.

nape The base of the neck at the back, where the top bone of the spine juts out.

neutral Not active, neither one thing nor the other, colourless.

non-fray(able) Opposite of frayable (see frayable).

notches 'V' shapes cut into the edge of the fabric used for joining pieces together.

numerous Many

omit(ting) leav(e)(ing) out

one-way design A pattern with a definite up and down to it, eg, flowers all growing in one direction.

open seam Two garment sections are joined RS together, with one row of stitching; the seam turnings are pressed open on WS.

overcasting A method of neatening edges; a thread is taken diagonally at even intervals over the edge of the fabric.

overlaid seam The upper section has one raw edge turned under and is then laid into the under section (matching fitting lines) and the layers stitched through.

overlap One piece is overlaid on to another.

overwhelming Too much to take

paisley-print A print with curved patterns; popular on quilt fabrics, men's dressing gowns and pyjamas; the design originated in India.

parallel Two lines at even distance from each other along their whole length.

parallelogram A mathematical, four-sided shape in which there are two pairs of parallel lines (a square is the simplest parallelogram).

Paris binding A straight binding used for seams and hem edges.

patch pocket One which is made up and applied to the garment on top of the fabric.

patchwork Small pieces of fabric of the same size (usually) and weight, but different colours and patterns, are stitched together to form a larger design or fabric.

pattern size The size of the pattern which is governed or influenced by the bust, waist and hip measurements.

penetrate Get through, pierce

perforations Little holes or cuts, often at the edge of a pattern.

perimeter The outside edge measurement

permutations Mixing and matching, 'ringing the changes'

petersham ribbon A ribbed ribbon with a slight lustre used for stiffening etc, eg, waistlines.

pile Raised surface of tufts of threads cut to an even length, eg, velvet, or left uncut, eg, towelling.

piped seam The seam is made up in the usual way but a piping strip is added between the seam join so that the seam is emphasized.

piping The straight grain or crossway strip used for all piped parts.

pleats A method of reducing fullness, whereby folds are taken into the fabric evenly down the length, and laid back over their own width on to the main garment.

plaid A woven pattern with different colour and width stripes going both horizontally and vertically.

polyamides A group of synthetic fibres, eg, *Nylon, Perlon, Banlon*

polyesters A group of synthetic fibres, eg, *Terylene, Trevira, Terlenka*, etc.

polyurethanes A group of synthetic fibres, eg, *Lycra, Spanzelle*.

pre-shrunk The fabric or garment has been shrunk before being sold or made up so that it will not shrink again when washed.

previous(ly) That which came before, former

procedure Method or order of work

properties The different qualities something has

proportions Parts of, parts in relation to each other

puckering Rucking up, gathering into folds

puff(ed) sleeve One which has fullness gathered into a band at the arm and at armhole; it usually finishes above the elbow.

pupa A stage of metamorphosis which the worm (of moth or butterfly) turns into (see cocoon).

raglan sleeve One which has a diagonal seam at the armhole going right up to the neck; there is no shoulder seam usually (unless going from neck to wrist).

rectangle A four-sided mathematical shape which has all its angles at right angles and its sides parallel, the two horizontal sides are of equal length as are the two vertical sides; the vertical length can be different from the horizontal length.

regenerated fibres Made with something else as the base, eg, regenerated cellulosic – *Rayon*.

regulator Thing which alters or changes something else.

reinforced Strengthened

resilient Able to resume its original shape

resistant Holds out against

retain(ing) Keeps, holds on to

retention Keeping to the original, holding power

right angles Angles of exactly 90°

rouleau(x) Tube(s) of fabric with the raw edges enclosed

scaled down A smaller version of the original

scalloped With even, curved edges, like a shell

scorched Fibres burned so they char but do not burst into flame

scuff Scratch or mark

seam allowance The amount allowed between the fitting line and the raw edges of a seam.

seam rolls Padded tubes for pressing over when pressing seam joins.

seam width Same as fell; the width of the finished seam.

self-facing A facing made of the same fabric

selvedge The warp threads at each side of the fabric as it comes off the bale; they are tighter or firmer than the rest.

set-in sleeve One which has an armhole seam following the natural line of the shoulder joint.

sequence Order of things

shank The raised lump at the back of a button

sheer Very fine, to the point of being transparent

shirring Gathering up the fabric evenly with many rows of thread.

sleeve head The crown or top of the sleeve where the full part that goes over the upperarm and shoulder joins the shoulder seams.

slubbed Having raised bumps every so often; made by taking one thread across more than one underneath or by twisting the thread unevenly during the spinning process; sometimes slubs are formed naturally in linens and silks.

sombre Dark, subdued

sophisticated Adult, grown up, smart

spinnerets The machines which spray drops of chemicals which harden into synthetic fibre chips (later made into fibres).

spiral A concentric circle, ie, starting from the centre and going round and round in ever increasing circles in a continuous line.

staple fibres Tiny filaments which can be spun into a crimped yarn, eg, *Crimplene*.

static electricity Natural electricity caused by friction of certain fabrics or fibres with other materials (seen as blue sparks in the dark).

stay stitching Stitching with a row of machining outside the fitting line of any edges which are likely to stretch before being made up.

steam iron An iron which can be filled with water; it has holes on the ironing surface where the steam comes out – this helps to press the fabric.

straight grain Following the line of the warp or the weft threads

straight stitch A machine stitch which has no width

stylized Geometrically shaped, very unrealistic looking

subjected to treated like, made to

subtle Cleverly done in an almost unnoticeable way – the finished effect being good usually.

surplus Extra

susceptible Likely to fall for, liable to be influenced by

swing needle A machine needle which moves from side to side as well as up and down.

synthetic Entirely man-made

tailor(ed)(ing) A method of making clothes where each section is finished professionally and backed or padded with stiffening to make it look crisp and smart.

tailor's chalk A piece of chalk used for marking fabrics

tailor's hams Very firmly padded ham-shaped pieces of fabric (like cushions) which are used for pressing darts etc.

tailor's tacks A method of taking marking, using double thread

taper(ed)(ing) off Trailing off to nothing at one end

taut Tight or at tight tension

techniques Special methods

temporarily Lasting only for a short time

tendency Having an inclination to

tension The tightness or looseness of something

texture(d) Having surface interest or depth

thonging Very thin strips of leather etc

three-dimensional Having a roundness or shape other than flatness

toile A mock up of the garment or pattern made in cheap, plain fabric; all alterations are done on this first before being transferred to pattern.

trait A personality tendency

transferred Changed across to

transparent See-through

triang(le)(ular) Three-sided

tricot Knitted

trim angles Clip across angles diagonally so they lie flat when turned through.

true cross At an angle of 45° to the straight grain

tuck(s)(ed) Folds taken into fabric and stitched down evenly along their length but not stitched down to main fabric; they are pressed in one direction.

turning allowance As seam allowance

twill weave Where the weft threads are woven in such a way as to give a diagonal look to the weave, eg, denim.

undersection The underneath piece

unostentatious Not too bright or garish

unravel Unpick, fray

variations Changes, alternatives

vertical Upright

voile(s) Sheer cotton(s)

warp The threads running up and down fabric parallel to selvedge.

weave The way threads are woven together.

weft The threads running across at right angles to the selvedge.

weight distribution The way the weight of something is portioned out.

welt pocket Like a bound pocket but with a flap stitched upwards.

yarn Thread

yoke The part of a garment which goes across the shoulders, back and front, up to neckline.

zig-zag A stitch with width, made by swing needle machines.

Index